Highland Trails

A GUIDE TO SCENIC
WALKING AND RIDING TRAILS

Northeast Tennessee
Western North Carolina
Southwest Virginia

Revised Edition with New Trails

Kenneth Murray

The Overmountain Press

JOHNSON CITY, TENNESSEE

— COVER PHOTOGRAPH —
Rhododendron in bloom at Grassy Ridge on the Appalachian Trail

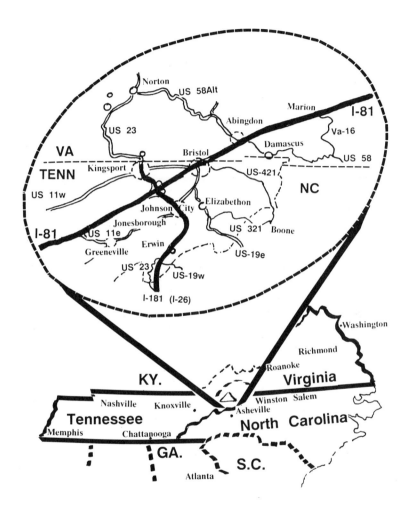

Back country and mountain trail travel can be dangerous. Trips on any of the routes described in this book are strictly at your own risk.

Walking on the Highlands of Roan, along the North Carolina/Tennessee border

— OTHER BOOKS BY KENNETH MURRAY —

DOWN TO EARTH — PEOPLE OF APPALACHIA
A PORTRAIT OF APPALACHIA
FOOTSTEPS OF THE MOUNTAIN SPIRITS — APPALACHIA*

*Scheduled for release November 1992 by
The Overmountain Press
325 West Walnut Street
P.O. Box 1261
Johnson City, TN 37605

Contents

Introduction

Foot travel has been an important mode of transportation in the Appalachian Region for centuries and was probably the major one until the World War II era. Many isolated communities were once accessible only by horse trails and footpaths. Today the role of walking has nearly been reversed from this tradition.

With the advent of the automobile, trail bike, and other off-road vehicles, a person almost never has to walk farther than the garage or parking lot. The centuries-old network of trails and paths is rapidly being reclaimed by nature and man. The remaining footpaths offer excellent recreational opportunities for those interested in a pleasant afternoon walk, away from a high tech world, as well as for serious hikers in search of longer more arduous treks. Except for the popular and well-documented Appalachian Trail, information on locations and what to expect along the walkways of northeast Tennessee, southwest Virginia and western North Carolina is fragmented.

This guidebook aims to consolidate as much of the material as practical, offering locator maps, photographs and firsthand observations on walking each trail. Estimated time or distances and degree of difficulty are included. There is a bias favoring the more easily traversed routes with outstanding visual appeal.

It is uncertain when the first people wandered onto the Appalachian Highlands, but it was at least twelve thousand years ago. These early hunter-gatherers probably followed game trails along the valleys and ridge crests. Even after settling into semi-permanent villages and adding farming to their livelihoods, the Woodland Indians of the Southern Appalachians had minimal impact on the environment. Although the valleys of the mountainous region covered in this guidebook were once populated by ancestors of the Cherokees, Catawbas, Shawnees, or unknown tribes, at the arrival of the first European explorers, most of the interior region was a vast no-man's-land. The Indian nations around the foothills used it as a hunting preserve, and possibly as a buffer region between hostile groups.

Early European visitors who left written records of the verdant highlands most often described the inter-mountain region as a pristine Garden of Eden. The climactic forest, where every species of plant and animal attained its maximum growth, extended as a great sea in seemingly endless waves for as far as the eye could see. Walking under the arching canopy of mammoth

Testing the water along the Little Stoney Creek Trail in the Jefferson National Forest.

trees was an experience likened to being in an enormous cathedral.

The forest that once covered this region is difficult to imagine. It must have been similar to the giant redwood stands of the West, but with a much greater variety of species.

Chestnut trees were the monarchs of the Appalachian forest, rivaling the redwoods in age and height. Chestnut and acorn mast supported large flocks of turkeys and herds of deer and supplemented the diets of other animals. Wood from the trees was durable, strong and fine grained. The loss of this species due to an imported blight early this century rates as one of the world's great botanical disasters.

Giant tulip poplars, dug out for canoes, could carry twenty men and their gear along unfettered rivers. There are reports of great hollowed-out trees being used as temporary homes or barns during the pioneer era.

Settlements and farmsteads in this vast wilderness were a long way from the manufacturing centers. Forests provided major sources of income from hunting, timbering and raw materials. In this land of make-do or do-without, wood was turned into hundreds of uses by characteristic Appalachian inventiveness, from paving for roads to water pipes and charcoal for smelting iron ore. But much of the great forest was squandered in slash and burn agriculture.

Today, there is almost no part of the Appalachian region that has truly virgin forest. Even the most remote areas have been at least selectively cut for their more valuable timber, such as walnut and cherry.

The wildlife was so plentiful that great herds of buffalo, elk and deer appeared to be one giant pulsating beast as they moved through the valleys or across meadows on the highlands. DeSoto's troop was presented several hundred turkeys by one foothills Indian village. Daniel Boone reportedly killed more than 2,500 deer and 100 bears, mostly for the skins, in one season, and he was only one of many such "Long hunters" in the lands between the Blue Ridge and Cumberland Mountains. More than 50,000 pelts per year were shipped through the port of Charleston alone during this era. Herds of eastern bison, now extinct, were slaughtered by the thousands by hunters from New Orleans; only their tongues, a delicacy in the city's restaurants, were taken. Flocks of carrier pigeons darkened the sky like vast clouds, but these chicken or grouse-size birds were harvested by the ton, also to extinction. Wildlife such as the eastern white tail deer, black bear and wild turkey is rebounding from these excesses in protected areas. Since hunting is now controlled, the major threat to the natural world comes from habitat loss through unregulated development.

Along the region's trails, worn smooth by centuries of use, Indian runners reportedly could cover 100 miles in a day, and youths could capture deer by chasing them until the prey was exhausted. Most of these woodland avenues, along with those blazed by pioneers like Boone, have been paved over to become the major highways through the valleys and mountain passes. The trails that remain are through more isolated hollows and less commercially valuable or accessible ridges. Most paths included here are through national forests, but even these are increasingly threatened by competing political pressures from timber and development interest. Perhaps greater use by those taking the time to travel the highlands on foot, and awareness of the vulnerability of these last remnants of our heritage, will promote their protection.

Today's trails are rarely the shortest distance between points, but they offer splendid vistas and the woodland serenity of a timeless Appalachia. Here is a reminiscence of more simple, earthy times.

Rain clouds and fog cover the valleys viewed from Unaka Mountain.

From the exalted highlands, modern complexities can be exchanged for a brief bond with the countless spirits that have passed before.

Some Basics

Area Covered

The trails in this guidebook are generally presented from south to north.

Most of the walks in this guide are within a one hour drive from northeast Tennessee's Tri-Cities region. The area covered is limited at the north by Virginia Highway 16, in the Mount Rogers National Recreation Area, and at the south by Tennessee Highway 70, in the Cherokee National Forest, east of Greeneville, Tennessee. The eastern edge is along the ridges that separate Tennessee and North Carolina, and the western edge is bounded by the Jefferson National Forest in Lee and Wise Counties in Virginia.

Back-country horseback riding and mountain bicycling are growing sports, and many of the trails listed in this guidebook are suitable for non-motorized use. However, designated horse trails vary considerably in the level of skill required, and each user must determine the appropriateness of the listed routes. Most sections of the national forests have closed timber, fire control, and off-road vehicle tracks that are open to horse and mountain bike travel. Unless there is a hiker-only notice, a trail may be used for non-motorized travel.

All of the Appalachian Trail, and most National Recreation Trails in this region, are restricted to foot travel only.

Trail Markings and Designations

The region hosts approximately 220 miles of the Appalachian Trail. The popular Maine to Georgia route, in addition to being the longest continuously marked footpath (2,135 miles), is also the best marked and maintained of the routes listed. Most marked paths now adopt its system of painted blazes.

The Appalachian Trail is marked with white painted blazes, approximately three by six inches vertically, placed on trees, rocks or set post. These blazes on clearly defined paths are rarely more than 100 yards apart and are usually much closer. Should you travel more than ¼ mile without seeing a white trail marker, a turn has probably been missed, and backtracking to pick up the main route is advised. A double white blaze is intended to get the hiker's attention. This is to warn of sharp or obscure turns in the path or other obstacles in the path and to alert the walker of approaching junctions.

Blazes of other colors or shapes denote intersecting trails or secondary routes. Blue painted blazes are frequently used to mark shorter spurs to springs, other water sources, or shelters, but are also used to mark some of the major trails. Other shapes such as diamonds or circles are used for some major trails. Occasionally, stacked rocks (similar to the system popular in the west) are used to mark sections of trail.

You may encounter one possible point of confusion concerning painted blazes—red or yellow markings are frequently used to mark the boundaries of wildlife management areas and National Forest lines, but these are usually accompanied with written notices, or include rings painted around the trees (in addition to the vertical blazes).

Better managed trails use the system described for the Appalachian Trail, with variations in color. Signs noting access points, road crossings and trail distances also help resolve confusion. Such improvements to guide the hiker are luxuries in many areas, however. For our purposes here, trails with painted or other markings (including those maintained and easily defined in other ways) will be considered primary routes. Those without such improvements will be listed as primitive or secondary routes.

Travel should be kept to the designated trails. Cutting across switchbacks may contribute to erosion on steep terrain. Also, in dense woods landmarks may be difficult to spot, especially in poor weather, and it is easy to become disoriented or to mistake deer trots or other wildlife paths for unmarked routes. A good map and compass are always recommended. When exploring primitive or secondary trails, extra time should be allotted for wrong turns, dead ends and backtracking.

Difficulty Ratings

Difficulty ratings for trails in this guidebook are reasonably self-explanatory. Any rating system is subjective, but the bias here is in favor of the casual hiker or day tripper. For a trail to be designated **"Easy,"** it is well defined, preferably marked, and offers few obstructions or severe grades. However, woodland walks are rarely without some challenge, due to uneven terrain and loose surfaces and usually require more effort than paved sidewalks.

A **"Moderate"** rating means the route, while a clearly defined path, is more difficult and probably requires some climbing. These routes are apt to be unmarked or less traveled, perhaps with creek crossings or other minor hazards.

A trail that carries a **"Difficult"** rating in this book would probably be called moderate by ardent hikers, and their "Difficult" I might decline to attempt. Routes that are poorly defined or that demand long, arduous climbs over steep or rocky terrain might also be put into this category. Scaling cliffs, rappeling, and other mountain climbing skills are left to the more adventurous.

Furthermore, conditions might change on any given route. This region is among the highest in annual rainfall, and unused or poorly maintained footpaths may erode or rapidly be reclaimed by forests. Logging, ownership changes, and development may also alter, close, or eliminate routes. On the other hand, demand for recreational opportunities are growing, and many hiking trails and access points are being upgraded within the national forests.

Equipment Needed

No special equipment is needed to enjoy this sport, but a good pair of hiking boots is recommended. Regular streetwear, or shoes designed for other activities, will do, but the combination of rocky terrain, poor traction, and improper foot and ankle support can cause falls and sprains, or at least very tired feet and legs. Sturdy boots with a good sole will eliminate many potential problems and enhance enjoyment of the scenery.

Any well-made hiking, hunting or work boot with a good all-terrain tread will serve quite well, but spongy synthetics or leather soles should be avoided. Combat-type boots and those with ventilated panels for warm weather are fine. Running shoes, or fabric sneakers, although cooler in summer, should be left to more even surfaces.

Two pairs of socks (or thin liners) are also a good idea, to absorb part of the friction between boot and skin and provide insulation in cold weather. Allowances for the extra bulk should be made when fitting footwear.

"Moleskin," available in foot care centers, can be applied to sensitive areas for added protection from blistering on longer hikes.

Other useful items: A simple compass, a map of the area being walked, a canteen, and water purification tablets. (The water in tumbling streams may be safe to drink, but sadly many water sources have unseen contaminants.) Carry enough water for your excursion or treat all water used along the way, no matter how sparkling it looks.

Everything needed for a day walk, including a snack, can be held in a belt-type or other small pack, or in a shoulder bag. It is also considerate to allow extra space in the pack to carry out the inevitable "Bud" can and "Twinkies" wrapper left along the path by unfortunates who had poor role models.

Safety Tips

- Hike with someone, but avoid large groups.

- Tell friends or family where you are going, and give them your anticipated time of return.

- Be prepared for severe weather by taking rain gear in summer and extra clothing in winter. Watch for sudden changes in the weather. DO NOT rely on regional weather forecast.

- Spot area landmarks before heading into wilderness areas, and stay on designated trails.

- A snakebite kit may be a worthwhile choice during warm weather. Poisonous snakes are seldom seen, and bites are unlikely through heavy fabrics or leather footwear, but watch where you are stepping and never put your hands or feet where they can't be seen. Reptiles love to sun themselves on rocky ledges in spring and fall or retreat from summer heat into rocky shelves or outcrops. Contrary to popular belief, snakes frequently do not run away at the approach of people; they are more apt to freeze where they are, relying on camouflage or stealth to hide them.

- Lyme Disease and Rocky Mountain Spotted Fever are recently added concerns, since ticks bearing these ailments may be present in the region, although there are few confirmed cases. The best protection from these creatures is to wear light colored long trousers tucked into the tops of boots or socks. They can then be seen crawling up the pants and intercepted. Also, daily checks of the scalp reduce the risk, so do repellent collars for pets.

- Wear brightly-colored clothing during hunting season, including a hunter's blaze orange cap and/or bib. Regulations require that at least 100 square inches of blaze orange be worn by anyone in some hunting areas during open season. Some recreational trails and wildlife management areas may be closed to loaded firearms, bows, weapons, and pack stock; other restrictions may be imposed as well, although hunting by permit is allowed in most of the national forests.

- Drink only boiled or treated water.

- Each person must take responsibility for his/her own safety when entering the forest. Plan your trip carefully, allowing plenty of time for crossing rugged terrain and for meeting the unexpected. It is easy to underestimate how much energy is required along mountainous trails.

Permits

No permits are needed by hikers for areas covered in this book. More heavily used areas of the Smokies, to the south, require permits, and registration for back-country campers and limits are imposed. Where designated trails cross private lands, stay on the path right-of-way.

Camping

Tent camping is allowed anywhere in the national forest along trails, and no permits or fees are required for backpackers except in developed campgrounds. Shelters are provided on heavily-used routes on a first come basis. When they are already taken, move further along the course to pitch your tent. Where routes pass through private lands, camp only in designated sites.

Backpack camping has another cost. Every ounce carried over the trail drains energy and enjoyment. For longer treks, the hiker should be in top physical condition and have above-average stamina.

When camping, aim for no impact on the environment and pack out all trash.

Facilities for RV's and camper trailers are available at controlled campsites only, and fees vary according to what is offered.

Campfires

Backpacker stoves are recommended, but if you build a fire, use only downed wood. Standing trees, even if dead, provide homes for woodpeckers, bees, squirrels and other wildlife. Open fires may be banned during dry weather, and care should be exercised never to leave the blaze unattended. Be certain it is completely out when you leave.

Do not build a fire under overhanging limbs or branches; build only a small blaze, well protected from any winds; and when leaving the campsite, remove any traces of your presence by scattering stone fire rings and ashes.

Campers may be liable for damages from wildfire.

Time and Distance Estimates

Time and distance estimates given in this guide are, in many cases, rough approximations. Where routes have been surveyed, accurate distances are possible, but due to variations in terrain, the twisting nature of many trails, and difference in individual walking speed, always allow extra time and energy.

Someone walking briskly with long legs might cover a mile in 15 minutes on sidewalks or paved roads. But in the woods, however, where one is going up hills, scrambling over rocks, fording streams and enjoying the scenery, the average hiker will do well to average two miles in an hour, or perhaps three miles per hour on easier routes.

Over steep terrain these are optimistic projections. Include time to enjoy the walk (since it should not be an endurance contest) as well as time to return to access points before nightfall, if not camping. After sundown in deep woods, it gets very dark very quickly, and night travel is not safe.

Due to variations in odometer calibrations, a ten percent variance should be allowed from road distances listed.

Seasons

Woodland hikes are to be enjoyed year-round in the Southern Appalachians, and each season has its special attractions.

Spring offers a profusion of wildflowers so numerous that even field guides rarely catalog them all. Trails that may be overgrown later in the growing season can still be easily followed.

The lushness of summer is the most popular recreational period, when vacationers swell the campgrounds. Most of the summer activity is around the lakes, parks and attractions that can be driven to, but weekends the more popular footpaths may be busy as well. Shorts, sneakers, and other summer wear are fine on the wider, heavily-used trails, but exposed skin and flimsy footwear invite problems with briars, stinging nettles, sunburn, poison ivy, mosquitoes and other insect bites, as well as blisters and bruises. Quiet walks can be found even during the busiest season on lesser-known routes and through the week.

Fall, even with the blazing display of colors, is relatively quiet along the trails until hunting season opens with a frenzy in areas with large deer populations. The brilliance of the leaves can last a month or more, as the scarlet, orange, yellow and russets descend with the frost from the higher elevations and ridge faces. The peak color migrates from ridge to ridge, depending on the species present, altitude, and exposure to winds and diminished daylight. In late autumn, fallen leaves may partially hide lesser-used paths and make for slippery footing. Extra precautions (such as brightly colored clothing to distinguish the hiker from wildlife) may also be needed for safety.

Winter suspends woodland activities for the majority, but most of the season is very pleasant hiking weather. Lower humidity and barren trees of the colder months open up many views that are veiled the rest of the year. Wildlife tracks are revealed in abundance, especially along streams.

If one dresses sensibly and avoids the steeper routes, walking, even when there is snow on the ground, can be as rewarding in winter as in other seasons. Close attention must be paid to changes in weather conditions (to avoid severe storms) since hypothermia and frostbite are real threats.

Finally

Every effort has been made in the compilation of the trail data in this guide to insure that the information is up-to-date and accurate. I have walked most of the trails recently, but I have also relied on maps and other available guidebooks, plus information from other hikers.

The book does not come with a guarantee, so each person must always use caution and common sense when exploring the routes listed. Conditions along a trail may change; in time a trail may be rerouted entirely. However, this guidebook can be a useful tool or starting point when locating and enjoying this region's more scenic offerings.

The Southern Appalachian highlands offer some of the best hiking country anywhere. Enjoy it and protect it.

Greene Mountain Area

Margarette Falls Trail, Bullen Hollow Trail, Phillips Hollow Trail, Greene Mountain Trail, connections with the Appalachian Trail and others.

The Greene Mountain area offers several hiking and multiple-use trails, as well as connecting paths to the Appalachian Trail. Trails in this chapter are within the Cherokee National Forest.

They range from short, scenic walks as the Margarette Falls route, to more demanding hikes like the Bullen Hollow or Camp Creek treks. Combined with walks in the nearby Horse Creek, Round Knob and Old Forge Recreation Areas, several circuit routes and longer hikes linked with the Appalachian Trail can be planned for itineraries of an afternoon to a week or more.

General orientation: The Appalachian Trail travels along the crests of the Bald Mountains that divide Tennessee and North Carolina in this region. Trails in this chapter, and the following Horse Creek, Round Knob and Old Forge sections, are along the western slopes of these summits. Trails and access points along eastern and northern slopes of these high ridges are listed in the following Appalachian Trail segments from the Devil's Fork/Rocky Fork area, southwest of Erwin.

Map for this area is on page 188.

How to Get There

Close attention must be paid to the few landmarks and distances to locate trail heads in this area. Road signs and route markings are inconsistent along county routes.

Access to the area is from Tennessee Route 107, approached from Johnson City, Jonesborough, or Erwin, from the north; or Tusculum and Greeneville, from the south.

Trails in the Horse Creek, Round Knob and Old Forge areas also follow directions in Access 1.

Access 1: Lower Greene Mountain Trails
Margarette Falls, Davis Creek, Bullen Hollow and Phillips Hollow Trails

From Johnson City: The most direct route is by Route 67 west to its intersection with Tennessee Route 81, at Lamar School (Jonesborough is to the right from this intersection and is 7.8 miles to the 11-E junction). Turn left, toward Erwin, and Route 107 is intersected in 0.8 mile, just across the Nolichuckey River. Turn west onto TN-107 (a right turn marked by a sign to Tusculum).

Drive 13.8 miles from the TN 81/107 juncture, then turn left toward the Horse Creek Recreation Area. There is a wooden Forest Service sign at this paved county road. At 0.8 mile turn right at Broyles Road (marked by a street sign), then right again, almost immediately, onto Greystone Road. (Note: Continuing straight at this intersection leads to the Horse Creek and Old Forge areas.)

Greystone Road is a narrow, winding, thinly paved lane with numerous side roads, and is heavily traveled. Note the intersection at 3.9 miles from the Broyles Road turn: This graveled Forest Service Road leads up the mountain to Round Knob Area Trails, including the **Cowbell Hollow, Davis Creek** and **Appalachian Trail** connectors. Pay close attention here, because the turn for trails on the lower part of Greene Mountain is the next narrow road, 0.2 mile on the left. There is a small sign to the Shelton Mission Church, and the narrow lane is paved.

From the turn onto Shelton Mission Road, the **Davis Creek Trail** is passed at 1.4 miles. This trail has a small wooden sign, noting that it was constructed by the U.S. Youth Conservation Corps in 1978, and there is turnout parking beside the road. This footpath follows the hollow to the Round Knob area, approximately 2.8 miles up the mountain. This trail is moderate to above average in difficulty, with several stream crossings and considerable moderately-rated climbing.

Continuing past the Davis Creek Trail access, the picturesque Shelton Mission Church is passed and the road becomes gravel. A small bridge is crossed, and the **Bullen Hollow Trail** sign is on the left, 2.4 miles from Greystone Road. The Bullen Hollow track (beginning as a wide jeep road) leads about ½ mile through the woods to a junction with the **Margarette Falls** and **Phillips Hollow Trails** near the first stream forks. There is a wooden sign at the end of the old road marking the junction.

At the stream fork, blue painted blazes mark the **Phillips Hollow Trail** on the opposite bank of the main stream. It follows the larger cascading creek up the mountain and ends at the **Appalachian Trail** in 2.7 miles. Beside the smaller, right branch of the creek, yellow painted vertical blazes mark the **Margarette Falls Trail**. The **Bullen Hollow Trail**, designated by yellow, diamond shaped, metal blazes nailed to trees, branches to the right about 100 yards before reaching the end of the old road and climbs diagonally up

Frozen Margarette Falls, an easy-rated walk on the Margarette Falls Trail.

the ridge. The Bullen Hollow Trail is a designated motorcycle route.
is easily overlooked, but it follows the ridge upward while the other
continue along the streams.

From Greeneville: TN 107 turns east from U.S. Highway 11-E at Tusculum;
the turn for Horse Creek Recreation Area is noted with a sign on the right
side of the roadway.

✗ no biking

Access 2: Upper Greene Mountain Trails
Greene Mountain, Camp Creek, Bullen Hollow and Appalachian
Trail connectors.

To reach the upper ends of trails started at Access 1 and additional higher
routes, continue driving along Shelton Mission Road from the Bullen Hollow
turn for 0.2 mile. Turn left onto the gravel road beside the Mountain Market,
and a paved road is reached in 2.4 miles. Turn left, pass Camp Creek School,
then turn left again beside a rock church, at 1.1 miles. From the church,
Forest Service Route 98 begins in one mile where the pavement ends. There
is a Cherokee National Forest sign at this point.

Traveling on Route 98 up Greene Mountain is a thrilling experience by
itself. The one-track forest road has a better surface than most, but there
are stretches with sheer drops off the side of the mountain with no guard
rails and rare spots for vehicles to meet safely. Take it easy and use the turnouts to do your sight-seeing. The views are great. Forest fires, in 1941 and
again in the 1980's, have defoliated the slopes, leaving unobstructed vistas.
Set by arsonists, the fires devastated a large area.

The **Greene Mountain Trail** is on the left, 3.5 miles from the National
Forest entrance. The trail is noted with a sign and yellow metal diamond
markers. There is parking for a couple of cars.

The intersection of Forest Service Route 42 is one more mile. Turn left
up the mountain and travel 4.6 miles, by a very rough single track road,
to the intersection with USFS-358.

The gate for Route 358 is usually open. This road dead ends in about 1.6
mile, and meets trails from lower on the mountain. At 0.8 mile along
USFS-358 the left branch, 358A, (with closed gate) is noted, and yellow
diamond blazes of trails from lower on the ridge are visible leading west
along the road. A turnaround/parking is reached in another 0.8 mile.
Converging on this circle, yellow diamonds of the **Greene Mountain and
Bullen Hollow Trails** emerge from the woods, along with an unmarked trail
with barriers, the **Camp Creek Trail**. From the 358/358A loop, the combined

yellow marked paths can also be seen continuing east. They meet USFS-42 after about one mile through the woods.

Returning to the 358/42 junction: Continuing up the mountain on USFS-42, the terminus of above trails is reached in 0.7 mile, with roadside parking. The old Viking Mountain Resort is 1.5 miles, and a turnaround is reached in another 0.8 mile, just below the old fire tower on Camp Creek Bald. The heavily vandalized tower still offers excellent panoramas. There is a forest of radio and microwave stations on this knob, including the Channel 39 transmitter.

The Appalachian Trail bypasses the summit on the south side of the ridge. There are short, primitive side trails connecting with the white blazed trail.

Heading off Greene Mountain: The routing in Access 2 can be followed in reverse, but for a closer route back to area towns, travel southwest from Camp Creek Bald on USFS-42 and continue 1.7 miles beyond the USFS-98 junction to Tennessee Route 70. Tennessee 70 leads west to Greeneville in about 15 miles.

Access 3:
Appalachian Trail at Allen Gap, on TN 70/NC 208; Appalachian Trail from Rocky Fork Road, NC 212; and Alternate Highway Routes.

Tennessee Highway 70 leads east from Greeneville to Allen Gap on the North Carolina line. The turn for USFS-42 has a sign, noted above in Access 2, and is passed near the top of the mountain. The **Appalachian Trail** crosses the highway at 0.3 from the TN-70/USFS-42 junction, just before reaching the State Line Cafe. There is a small sign, visible white blazes, and turnout parking beside the roadway.

The highway becomes North Carolina 208 at the border. To reach access points along the eastern slopes of the Bald Mountains, continue east on 208/70 for 5.8 miles, then turn northeast onto paved NC-212, noted with a sign to Rocky Fork. The **Appalachian Trail** is crossed again in 14.6 miles. There is turnout parking beside Route 212, and white trail blazes are visible.

This route becomes TN-352 and meets U.S. Highway 23 in 4.4 miles from the trail crossing.

Margarette Falls Trail
Trail distance: 1 mile, one way.
Difficulty rating: Easy.

The Margarette Falls Trail is a short, fairly easy walk terminating at the falls. Only slightly more than one mile from the county road, almost half the distance to the falls can be driven in vehicles with high ground clearance. The remainder of the route is well marked with yellow painted blazes.

Beginning at Shelton Mission Road (see Access 1), the walk is along an old jeep track through woods choked with wild grape vines and laurel thickets. The stream is to the left. After a nearly level ½ mile (estimated) walk, there is a sign noting the **Phillips Hollow/Margarette Falls Trails** junction, at the end of the old road.

The Margarette Falls route turns right, following the smaller branch. Until recently, the path from the stream fork would have fallen into the primitive trail category, but recent upgrading by the Forest Service has added yellow painted vertical blazes and removed obstructions as fallen trees.

The remaining 0.6 mile to the scenic falls is a single file path that is slightly more difficult that the rough road section, except during periods of heavy rains when it may be impassable.

The stream has several small cascades as it tumbles from the heights. Mist from the splashing water covers the plants in the ravine, making the mosses and ferns a lush green. This verdant carpet contrasts sharply with sheer cliffs to the left of the stream; these cliffs present rocky strata which has been exposed for eons. Approaching the falls, the stony walls rise vertically for 75-100 feet. The hillside on the steep right bank is strewn with rocks and boulders.

The trail crosses back and forth through the creek, along stepping stones, and at one point marches right up the middle of the stream. The fords present no real hazards and the stream is shallow, even if you should slip. There are several smaller falls along the route, with pools that support native Brook Trout.

The Margarette Falls are at the end of the marked route. They cascade 60-75 feet into the narrow gorge.

Bullen Hollow Trail
Trail distance: 4 miles (estimated) one way.
Difficulty rating: Difficult. Steep, eroded, motorcycle designated route, poorly marked.

The Bullen Hollow Trail bypasses Margarette Falls to climb the rough ridge. Just before the junction of the Phillips Hollow/Margarette Falls Trails, a yellow metal diamond marker designates this trail turning from the rough road. This is reached before the stream forks.

Listed as a motorcycle trail on Forest Service maps, it is steep, eroded and rocky in sections. There are occasional diamond blazes, and the route is fairly wide and easily followed by those on foot, except for the climbing. The trail is not that heavily used, but bikers may be encountered on weekends, and care should be taken to keep out of their way. Above the falls and cliffs, the route crosses the stream from Reynolds Ridge to ascend the Henry Ridge spur of Greene Mountain. Due to unauthorized rerouting to avoid gullied-out sections, it is sometimes difficult to tell which is the main route. A topographical map and compass are recommended to stay on course when using this trail.

Reaching the mountain crest in roughly four miles, the track joins other area trails, the **Greene Mountain** and **Camp Creek Trails**, to converge on the knoll at Forest Service Road 358, Access 2. USFS Routes 358/358A make a loop around the knob. Yellow diamond markers leading generally west or southwest along this shoulder denote the Greene Mountain horse trail. An unmarked trail turning northwest from the circle is the old, mostly abandoned Camp Creek Trail. Continuing southeastward along the combined trails toward Camp Creek Bald and the Greene Mountain summit, USFS-42 is intersected in less than one mile.

Continuing walks could include connecting with the Appalachian Trail, traveling northward to the intersection with the Phillips Hollow Trail, and completing a circuit by following it back to the starting point, at Access 1.

Phillips Hollow Trail

Trail distance: 3.2, one way from Shelton Mission Road to junction with Appalachian Trail.
Difficulty rating: Moderate, but with climbing and fords.

From Access 1 the Phillips Hollow Trail begins on the opposite creek bank from the junctions of the Margarette Falls and Bullen Hollow Trails. The main creek is much wider and deeper than the small branch from Margarette Falls. Fording it may be unsafe during periods of heavy rains.

The route may be approached on the opposite bank from the bridge on Shelton Mission Road, but fords may be treacherous even as the stream diminishes in wet or snowy weather. There are only stepping stones at the creek crossings. The trail is well marked with blue vertical painted blazes, and the route is easily followed along the narrow hollow.

Initially the trail is along an old jeep or logging road and is fairly wide. The grade is fairly constant with steep sections. The **Artie Hollow Trail** is intersected at 1.8 miles above the Margarette Falls junction. The Artie Hollow

Trail turns eastward toward the Round Knob Area meeting the **Davis Creek Trail** (which climbs a parallel hollow) in about two miles; the distance uphill from the junction to Round Knob is another mile.

For the most part the Phillips Hollow Trail follows the tumbling stream. There are small falls, cascades and pools in the stream, and the route is particularly colorful in the fall, since there are numerous maples mixed with the poplar, buckeye, hickory and other hardwoods. The route is not used regularly, and while it is clear enough most of the year, it may be overgrown in summer.

White blazes of the **Appalachian Trail** are met on the summit 2.7 miles from the Margarette Falls Trail junction. A right turn onto the Appalachian Trail leads about two miles to Camp Creek Bald (although jeep roads turn away from the marked route for meadows at the Viking Mountain property in about 1.5 miles).

Going north on the Appalachian Trail, you will reach the old road descending to Round Knob in about two miles.

Greene Mountain Trail
Trail distance: 3.7 miles.
Difficulty rating: Easy to Moderate.
Horse/Mountain Bike Use.

The Greene Mountain Trail is a designated horse trail. Tracks of trail bikes may also be seen along the route. It is a wide and easily followed route with occasional yellow metal diamond blazes nailed to trees. Most of the grades are gradual as the route leads along the crest of the shoulder of the mountain. The route begins high on the ridge, so there isn't nearly as much climbing here as routes beginning lower in the valleys.

Much of the route is through scrubby pines and regrowth forest. There are screened views, but few open sections.

Round Knob Recreation Area

The Round Knob picnic shelter is nearly five miles from Greystone Road (see Access 1 on page 13). Trails crossing the point include the **Davis Creek, Cowbell Hollow,** and **Big Jennings Creek** and **Little Jennings Creek Trails.** The **Appalachian Trail** lies at the end of the jeep road that continues beyond the site.

View from the Round Knob area near heads of Davis Creek and Cowbell Hollow Trails.

Map for this area is on page 189.

Round Knob Trail
Trail distance: 3 miles, estimated, one way.
Difficulty rating: Moderate.
Appalachian Trail Connector.
Horse/Mountain Bike Use.

The Round Knob Trail follows the old road that once made a loop to the summit of the Bald Mountains and then ran back along Horse Creek. Beginning at the Round Knob picnic shelter parking area, it is now used as a rough jeep road and horse trail when the gate is open. The eroded track is fairly easy walking, but there are steep grades and loose rocks.

At about 2½ miles from the shelter parking, a turnaround and barriers end the jeep/horse route. There are notices barring vehicle and horse use beyond that point.

The **Appalachian Trail** is intersected in another ½ mile as it traverses the crests. There is a weathered wooden sign marking the turn atop the mountain. A right turn from the junction leads to the **Phillips Hollow** and **Hickey Branch Trails**. Left along the white blazed route leads about one mile to the Jerry Cabin Shelter. The junction of the **Fork Ridge Trail** into the North Carolina Big Creek Area is reached about ¼ mile before the Jerry Cabin site. The **Horse Creek Trail** turns back down the Tennessee slope in another 2 miles.

Davis Creek Trail
Trail distance: 2.8 miles, one way.
Difficulty rating: Moderate to difficult.

The Davis Creek Trail is fairly easy to follow as it traces the stream most of its 2.8 miles from Shelton Mission Road to the picnic shelter at the Round Knob Recreation Area (see Access 1). The trail is blazed.

The path has a rise in altitude of around 1,000 feet, with grades slightly more moderate than the parallel Phillips Hollow route. The stream is also smaller, but there are several fords.

Approximately one mile from the Round Knob picnic shelter, the **Artie Hollow Trail** turns west to connect with the **Phillips Hollow Trail**.

The Davis Creek Trail is a pleasant woodland walk along a tumbling branch. There is a sign at Round Knob noting the trail head. A path directly behind the shelter also descends to Davis Creek. The lower end of the trail, on Shelton Mission Road, is marked with a sign as well.

There is ample parking at the Round Knob picnic site. The **Cowbell Hollow** and **Big** and **Little Jennings Creek Trails** begin opposite the shelter.

Artie Hollow Trail
Trail distance: 2 miles, but access only by other trails.
Difficulty rating: Moderate.

The Artie Hollow Trail is a connector between the parallel climbing **Davis Creek** and **Phillips Hollow Trails**. The route is fairly easy to follow, and it

Big Jennings Creek cascades into a small pool near its junction with the Cowbell Hollow and Poplar Cove Trails.

has signs at each end. It is a narrow footpath beside a small stream which has a small waterfall on the Davis Creek end. The middle section of the path becomes overgrown in summer.

Cowbell Hollow Trail
Trail distance: 1.5 miles, one way.
Difficulty rating: Moderate.
Horse/Mountain Bike Use.

The Cowbell Hollow Trail, a designated horse trail, is a clearly defined, easy to follow, moderate to easy walk. It begins with a sign opposite the Round Knob picnic area.

The **Little Jennings Creek Trail**, a more narrow footpath, turns left from the horse trail in 0.1 mile. This trail descends the ridge slope in a generally eastward direction along a developed, moderately graded, wide track. It passes through small pines and regrowth forest. The terminus of the Cowbell Hollow route is at 1.5 miles, at the junction of the **Big Jennings Creek Trail**.

Big Jennings Creek leads downstream to the Old Forge Recreation Area. The **Poplar Cove Trail** turns eastward toward the Horse Creek area in 0.3 mile along the Jennings Creek route; and the **Little Jennings Creek** route is intersected again near the Old Forge end.

Horse Creek Area

The Horse Creek Recreation Area has a well maintained system of trails. Mostly designated as horse trails, the routes are well defined and marked. The trails interconnect with off-road vehicle, motorbike and hiking trails of the Old Forge, Round Knob and Greene Mountain areas, in addition to the Appalachian Trail. They offer varied terrain, scenery and duration.

Part of the vista from "Big Rock" overlook near the meeting of the Horse Creek and Appalachian Trails.

Map for this area is on page 189.

How to Get There

The Horse Creek Récreation Area, with its trails and camping/picnic grounds, is reached from Tennessee Highway 107 in Greene County, Tennessee. There is a sign to the area beside the highway. From the turn, follow the paved road and signs for 2.8 miles to the park entrance. (See Access 1 in the Greene Mountain Section.)

Immediately after entering the National Forest reserve, the excellent gravel USFS-331 turns right toward the Old Forge Area (note for Old Forge connections). A large wooden map of the Horse Creek Recreation Area and its facilities is just ahead on the left.

To reach this area's trails, continue on paved USFS-94 (Horse Creek Road). The pavement ends in 0.2 mile at a parking area. Rough forest road 5094 continues beyond the parking and is passable with off-road vehicles, horses or on foot. This is the **Horse Creek Trail**.

The **Squibb Creek Trail** turns to the left at 0.2 mile from the pavement's end. It begins across a footbridge and has a prominent sign.

Continuing along the **Horse Creek Trail,** the **Poplar Cove Trail** turns westward in one mile, just after the fourth stream crossing (count them if you are interested in this route). **Pete's Branch** and **Sarvis Cove** hiker paths are reached via the Poplar Cove Trail, as well as the **Big Jennings Creek Trail** which connects with the Round Knob and Old Forge area trails.

The **Horse Creek Trail** continues on to the top of Rich Mountain as a wide, very steep old road, where it intersects the **Appalachian Trail.**

Horse Creek Trail ⚹
Trail distance: 4 miles, approximate, one way.
Difficulty rating: Moderate. 2,000 feet climb, mostly by gradual slope but with steep sections near top.
Connecting trails: Appalachian, Poplar Cove, Squibb Creek.
Horse/Mountain Bike Use.

The Horse Creek Trail is a multiuse route traveling from the campground of the same name to the top of Rich Mountain. Although not blazed, it is a wide, easily followed old road. As an off-road route, it has several stream crossings, few turnouts, and is suitable only for all-terrain machines, horses or foot travel.

As a hiking trail, it is well defined and rated easy to moderate on the lower part of the mountain. The ridge side is fairly steep, especially near the summit area. Creek fords, with stepping stones, are shallow except at flood stage. Several foot and horse trails turn off the main trail.

Beginning the walk at the gate, with the 5094 marker and paved parking area, the first marked side trail encountered is the **Squibb Creek Trail**. This is a much more challenging path than the Horse Creek Trail and makes a rough arc from the old road to emerge atop Rich Mountain. A sign and yellow painted blazes are visible.

Continuing along the Horse Creek road: The stream is crossed four times before reaching the next crossroads, roughly one mile from the paved parking. Just beyond the fourth creek crossing, the **Poplar Cove Trail** turns right and may be followed to explore the Pete's Branch Falls area, or to connect with Round Knob and Old Forge routes. It would be easy to take a wrong turn. (At the third ford, for instance, there is a wide trail turning right to scale the ridge; after about ¼ mile it deteriorates into a primitive, unmarked path. Sometimes used by hunters, it travels over the ridges to eventually reach Big Jennings Creek).

The **Poplar Cove** turn is distinguished by double yellow blazes. There were no signs my last trip, but it is a blazed trail, beginning as a single track road.

The Horse Creek Trail is the left branch of this fork and continues upstream, with switchbacks, along the unmarked single track road.

Nearing the top of the mountain, 3.7 miles from the pavement, an orange gate is encountered which is intended to end vehicular traffic, although it has been circumvented. There is a large turnaround at this gate. A small path to the right leads, less than one hundred feet, to an overlook. The view is worth the additional climb; from atop the rocky outcrop, one can see mountains layered upon mountains, spanning a 180 degree panorama to the north.

This precipice overlooks the country roamed by famed frontiersman Davy Crockett. His birthplace and family farmstead can be seen in the valleys to the northwest; it is probable that he hunted these ridges as a youth, perhaps even stood atop this same rocky face. (The Davy Crockett State Park, on the Nolichuckey River, which has a reconstructed Crockett homestead, is located between Jonesborough and Tusculum on U.S. 11-E; slightly farther west is the town of Greeneville, home of President Andrew Johnson. (The Andrew Johnson Homestead, tailor shop and visitors center is maintained by the National Park Service there.)

Visible to the northeast is Historic Jonesborough, Tennessee's oldest town, where Andrew Jackson practiced law as a young man. Also in this direction the Boones Creek area can be picked out; here, on one ocassion, Daniel Boone is supposed to have hidden from hostile Indians behind a waterfall. He is also supposed to have left an inscription on a beech tree commemorating killing a bear in the area. (The black bear has been hunted out of this area for several generations; although, they have been successfully reintroduced along the Tennessee/North Carolina highlands, and controlled hunts are once again allowed.)

This area of the Cherokee and Pisgah National Forests is reserved as a bear habitat. White tail deer, wild turkey and other wildlife are also plentiful along the Horse Creek Trail in the Rich Mountain area.

The rough Horse Creek Road continues diagonally up the ridge, from the orange gate and turnaround to near the summit and intersects another old single track road that travels along the crest.

The **Appalachian Trail** follows this old road, sometimes taking a detour through the woods to avoid bike and ATV tracks; this is the main path atop the mountain. To the left, from the Horse Creek junction, along the white blazed route, the nearby Big Rock butte stands at 4,838 feet. It has limited views of Tennessee on one side and North Carolina on the other. There are fairly open fields on this high point, and a side road to the left leads over a grassy meadow to a makeshift shed used by hunters and hikers. The terminus of the rough **Squibb Creek Trail** emerges from the thickets at this point, marked with blue blazes. Continuing north on the white blazed trail, the route turns more to the southeast from the peak, toward the Locust Ridge shelter and Devils Fork Gap (around 6.5 miles).

Turning right from the **Horse Creek/Appalachian Trails** junction, the infrequent white blazes generally follow the rutted road. Near the first clearing, if you look very closely, the double yellow blazes for the **Sarvis Cove Trail** heads down the mountain to the **Poplar Cove Trail**. It is only a few hundred yards to this turn. Continuing south with the ruts on the Appalachian Trail, there are fairly open grass and briar fields where the route meanders along the summit. The Jerry Cabin Shelter is in this segment. The old road to Round Knob turns sharply off the summit at around 2½ miles.

The Bald Mountains were covered throughout the range by grassy meadows and heath slicks long before there was a written history of the area. These Appalachian balds have been almost entirely reclaimed by forest or weeds and briars. The historical Bald Mountains are not bald anymore; the open vistas they once presented are now rare.

Poplar Cove Trail
Trail distance: 1.5 miles, estimated, one way.
Difficulty rating: Mostly easy.
Primarily a connector between Horse Creek, Round Knob and Old Forge area trails.
Horse/Mountain Bike Use.

The Poplar Cove Trail is designated as a horse trail and begins at just over one mile from the Horse Creek Recreation Area parking (see Horse Creek Trail). From the Old Forge Area, the trail is intersected in about one mile along the Big Jennings Creek Trail. It is only accessible by other trails.

Beginning on the **Horse Creek Trail** end: Look for the double yellow blazes just beyond the fourth crossing of the creek. The route is wide, well marked with yellow painted blazes, and has gradual slopes, although some climbing can be expected over the ridges. The lane parallels a trickle of a stream initially, but this is primarily a woodland walk over low ridges.

From the turn onto the Poplar Cove route, the **Pete's Branch Trail** turns left in less than ¼ mile from the Horse Creek departure. Also marked with yellow painted blazes, this trail turns immediately after crossing the first ford, then follows the larger branch of the stream. Pete's Branch Trail is a narrow footpath leading to a small waterfall.

Continuing up the grade on the Poplar Cove Trail, another fork is reached in ½ mile. Again, both trails are marked with yellow blazes. The left fork ascends the mountain via the **Sarvis Cove Trail**, which intersects the **Appalachian Trail** on the crest.

The right fork is the continuation of the Poplar Cove route, marked with both yellow metal diamonds and painted blazes in this section. From this junction the trail narrows and is slightly steeper.

The Jennings Creek Trail terminus of the route is reached in another mile. There is a weathered sign pointing downstream to Old Forge. Upstream leads to the Cowbell Hollow Trail and the Round Knob Recreation Area. Many of these routes can be linked together for all day excursions and circuit walks that return to Horse Creek.

Sarvis Cove Trail
Trail distance: 2.5 miles, estimated, one way.
Difficulty rating: Difficult—steep grade, poorly marked.
Appalachian Trail/Poplar Cove Trail connector.

The Sarvis Cove Trail turns left from the **Poplar Cove Trail** at about ¾ mile from the **Horse Creek Trail**. The trail connects with the Appalachian Trail on the summit. The lower portion of the route is wide and moderately easy, but becomes strenuous, poorly defined and narrow toward the top. The route generally travels toward the south or southeast, toward the crest, and is intermittently marked with yellow painted blazes. The lower head to the trail may also be approached from the **Big Jennings Creek Trail** via the **Poplar Cove Trail**.

From the Poplar Cove junction, the Sarvis Cove route follows an old forest road for about the first mile. A stream is crossed once in this section, but it is around one hundred yards below the old road for most of this distance. As the stream narrows, so does the trail, with the two joining as the grade becomes steeper. When the route begins some earnest climbing, closer attention must be paid to the trail blazes. They are farther and farther apart, and the route is reduced to single file as it passes beneath ancient hemlock trees.

Nearing the head of the hollow, the remaining trickle of a stream forks and the trail doubles back the opposite direction to climb the ridge. This sharp turn is at the edge of the grove of large hemlocks and could be easily overlooked. The trail is all hard climbing from here to the summit, along a serpentine course on the slope. From this point there are several fallen trees across the path adding to the difficulty. Yellow ribbons supplement the painted blazes up the ridge, but these are badly deteriorated. Before reaching the crest, the route appears uncertain at times, but pushing on toward the top it widens again, a couple of hundred yards below the rutted road along the summit.

Should the marked path be lost on the ridge side, the dry stream bed can be followed uphill. The day I climbed this trail, the ground was covered with snow and it was very foggy. I had little difficulty locating the blazes and even found a red ribbon noting the 4,200 feet level, although some looking around was required a couple of times. It would be easy to lose the path on the side of the mountain. A topographical map and compass is recommended, but if in doubt, the correct direction on this route is straight up and generally to the south. Additional care should be taken as you near the top, since there are large boulders and cliffs.

The road atop the summit follows the crest east and west, linking the Horse Creek and Round Knob Roads. The **Appalachian Trail**, with its white blazes, follows the old road much of the time in this area, although running parallel through the woods. A left turn from the Sarvis Cove/Appalachian Trail junction is north on the white trail, and the **Horse Creek Trail** is the next road turning from the summit.

Pete's Branch Trail and Waterfalls

The trail up Pete's Branch begins at the first stream crossing on the **Poplar Cove Trail**. The path is suitable only for foot travel, but it is well marked with painted yellow blazes along its ½ mile length.

The walk is fairly easy along the small stream, and although there are fords along the route, there is just barely enough water to get your feet wet.

The brook spills approximately 45 feet from the cliffs to a small pool at the base. The volume of water is divided into two thin ribbons and is reduced to nothing in dry weather. The falls may not be spectacular (except possibly during heavy rains) but still a refreshing, short diversion from the **Horse Creek** and **Poplar Cove Trails**.

Squibb Creek Trail ⚹

Trail distance: 4 miles, estimated.
Difficulty rating: Moderate within Recreation Area; Difficult on higher ridges.

Turning from the **Horse Creek Trail**, 0.2 mile from the parking area at the Horse Creek Campground, the Squibb Creek Trail is a moderately rated footpath for the first couple of miles. It begins at a footbridge across the creek and is well marked with yellow painted blazes until the boundary of the recreation area is reached. This foot-travel-only route takes a course roughly parallel with the multi-use Horse Creek Trail/USFS-5094 to the crest of Rich Mountain; however, it deteriorates to difficult on the steep upper slopes and goes over private holdings en route to the top.

Using a good topographical map and compass, the route can be followed to the crest, offering connections with several good trails on this shoulder of the mountain. These connecting routes include the old road that leads from the Cassi Creek area, which leads across Wilson Knob, to the other side of the mountain, where it descends along Higgins Creek to U.S. 23.

Old Forge Area

Map for this area is on page 189.

The Old Forge Recreation area lies between the Horse Creek and Round Knob areas. It is at the end of Forest Service Route 331, which turns right from Horse Creek Road just inside the Horse Creek Recreation Area entrance (see Horse Creek section).

En route to the Old Forge parking area the **Doctor's Ridge Trail**, with a horse trail sign, is at 1.9 miles. Other unmarked horse and off-road vehicle trails also turn from the gravel road in this area.

The Old Forge Recreation Area is reached in 2.8 miles. An area for tethering mounts is provided, as are picnic and primitive camp sites as well. The start of the **Big Jennings Creek Trail** is at the entrance to the parking area.

Small waterfall at the Old Forge Recreation Area near heads of Big and Little Jennings Creek Trails.

Big and Little Jennings Creek Trails
Horse/Mountain Bike Use.

The Big Jennings Creek Trail and Little Jennings Creek Trail both travel to the Round Knob Recreation Area from the Old Forge parking. The larger trail, up the larger creek, takes three miles (estimated) of mostly easy walking and connects with other area trails en route. The smaller stream route is also the shorter, at two miles (estimated), but is more difficult and more suited to foot travel. Both are listed as horse trails.

The trail head is marked at the entrance of the Old Forge parking area, just before the cattle guard/gate. Follow the yellow blazes around the picnic area. Just before crossing the stream at the first ford, a worthwhile 100 foot detour leads downstream to small falls and a pool behind the fence and clearing.

At the ford, steps lead down to the stream, which is easily crossed by skipping across the rocks. Just across the second ford, the **Little Jennings Creek Trail** turns up the smaller branch to the right. There has been a stone marker at this junction, but the rock slab on which it was lettered has been broken and sometimes lies beside the trail. At other times it is propped up, so it may not be there the next time someone needs its direction. The Little Jennings Creek Trail leads two miles to the Round Knob Recreation Area, where it joins the **Cowbell Hollow Trail** just before the parking area.

The **Big Jennings Creek Trail** is the path of least resistance as it makes its way along the larger stream and up the coolie. This route travels between the ridges and has a gradual slope. There are numerous opportunities to make a big splash as the trail crisscrosses the creek, but the rushing water is fairly shallow, rarely above knee deep.

Yellow painted blazes are frequently placed on trees, and the path is fairly wide and unobstructed.

Scenery along the creek is very pleasant with small cascades, chutes and quiet pools. An umbrella of laurel branches arch overhead in places. Sights and sounds of the forest stream envelop the walker along this path, filtering out all references to the world outside the wood.

The intersection of the **Poplar Cove Trail**, coming down the ridge from the left, is reached in about one mile. It is marked with yellow metal diamond markers and painted blazes. A weathered wooden sign at the junction points to the Old Forge and Round Knob sites. Continuing upstream on the Big Jennings Creek Trail, the **Cowbell Hollow Trail** is only another ¼ mile. There is a wooden sign at this junction, and the yellow marked main trail turns up the ridge for the Round Knob Area, becoming the Cowbell Hollow route.

For those who don't mind some bushwhacking and exploring, Jennings Creek can be followed upstream from the above junction by an unmarked trail. The first ½ mile is relatively easy, but the path becomes steep, the stream divides into smaller branches, and the going becomes difficult. The rough, primitive path might possibly be followed on to the summit area, but it would be a struggle.

From the Round Knob or Old Forge sites, the routes of the Big and Little Jennings Creek Trails combined with the Cowbell Hollow route make a pleasant half day circuit of approximately five miles.

Doctor's Ridge Trail
Horse/Mountain Bike Use.

Between the Horse Creek and Old Forge areas there are several horse and off-road vehicle paths turning into the woods from route 331. Most of these unmarked routes lead parallel to the gravel Forest Service road. Others (such as the Doctor's Ridge Trail) descend the ridge. It is marked with a horse trail sign on the right side of the road at 1.9 miles from Horse Creek Road. The route is wide and easily followed, but with some steep sections. The marked trail connects with the Greystone Road in 1.2 miles of woodlands.

To meet the trail from the Greystone Road end, turn from TN-107 at the Horse Creek Area sign. Turn right onto Greystone Road in just under one mile. The trail is 2.3 miles from this junction. There is a horse trail sign at this end of the trail, and orange Wildlife Management Area notices are placed along the roadway. There is parking off the road on this small hilltop, and the trail into the woods is wide and well defined.

Appalachian Trail

Allen Gap/Greene Mountain, north to Devil's Fork
Trail segment distance: 20 miles, one way.

Section overview:

Northward on the Maine to Georgia trail, the path straddles the state lines along the spine of the Bald Mountains chain. This trail segment offers an opportunity for a longer, uninterrupted trek through controlled woodlands and along the remaining balds and meadows of this range. There are no intersecting roads, but old logging tracks and multi-use trails approach the summit at several points, allowing shorter day hikes or circuit routes.

The difficulty rating of this long section is mostly easy to moderate, except for a long climb on the Greene Mountain end, ascending toward Camp Creek Bald.

This segment is divided into three parts, described below.

Section 1:
Appalachian Trail: North from Allen Gap to Camp Creek Bald—6 miles.

Map for this segment is on page 188.

Tennessee Highway 70/North Carolina 208 crosses the crest of the Bald Mountains at Allen Gap on the states borders, dividing Greene County, Tennessee and Madison County, North Carolina. There is a faded sign noting the Appalachian Trail crossing the highway. Turnout parking is beside the roadway. Nearby, on the North Carolina side of the crest, is the State Line Cafe. (Also, see Access Points from the Greene Mountain and Devils Fork/Rocky Fork areas.)

South on the trail from this gap leads to the Spring Mountain Shelter in 4 miles, the French Broad River at Hot Springs in 14.4 miles, and the Smokies in about 50 miles.

White trail blazes heading steeply up the bank and into the forest are easily spotted at the gap. The path in this area is through mixed public and private lands, but stays within the Pisgah and Cherokee National Forests most of the route. There is steady climbing on this shoulder of Camp Creek Bald;

the trail gains around 2,500 feet from the gap to the crest area, a distance of 6 miles.

Ascending the initial ridges from the gap, there are several unmarked old roads and side trails. At about one mile, gravel Forest Service Route 42 can be seen through the trees. Another old road connecting with USFS-42 is crossed in another 0.6 mile. This is the old Hayesville Road (to a community on the Tennessee side), and it intersects USFS-42 near the USFS-98 junction. The Little Laurel shelter is 4.9 miles from the highway. Near the shelter, another side trail leads northward to Route 42. Continuing with the white blazes toward Camp Creek Bald, the trail doesn't climb all the way to the summit, but skirts around its southern and eastern slopes to about 100 yards below the pinnacle.

Section 2:
Continuing Appalachian Trail: Camp Creek Bald north to Horse Creek Trail Junction—About 7.5 miles.

Map for this segment is on page 189.

There is a trail junction atop Camp Creek Bald, about 6 miles from Allen Gap. The right branch descends the North Carolina ridge to connect with the **Whiteoak Flats Trail, Pounding Mill Trail**, Shelton Laurel Road and NC-208. The left fork leads a short distance through scrubby, dwarfed growth to the old fire tower on the peak. These paths fall into the more primitive category, and can be partly obstructed. The fire tower is a short, sturdy structure dwarfed by the surrounding antennae farm atop the crest. The tower and its cabin have been heavily damaged by vandalism, so it remains to be seen how much longer the Forest Service will leave it on the high knob before pulling it down. Even with the other spires gracing the ridge, there are excellent 360-degree views from the fire tower deck. Without this vantage point the scenic views would be very limited. The tower also makes an excellent reference point for compass readings, since it is visible from the surrounding valleys and clear ridge lines.

The Viking Mountain Resort is on this summit. The facilities of this defunct time-sharing development pose silently on the crest awaiting resolution of the controversies surrounding them, which include ownership changes and suits of creditors and investors in the project. Stone gates with ''No Trespassing'' signs still intimidate travelers on the Forest Service right-of-way (USFS-42) near the high point. The peak and turnaround/parking are 0.8 mile beyond the Viking Mountain gates.

Road Access: A new sign beside TN-70 marks the turn of USFS-42 to Camp Creek Bald. It is the first gravel road on the Tennessee side of Allen Gap, and it is nine miles from the paved highway to the top of Camp Creek Bald.

After circling Camp Creek Bald, the Appalachian Trail skirts the meadows and development, then climbs the next ridge. About one mile past the resort development and about 8 miles from Allen Gap, an area of open views from high rocky cliffs is reached. Short side paths lead to White Rock Cliffs on the North Carolina side of the crest, and a bit further north to Blackstack Cliffs, for the Tennessee view. These two view points are noted with wooden signs a few hundred yards apart.

Part of the view into North Carolina from the White Rock Cliffs overlook on the Appalachian Trail, along the crest of the Bald Mountains.

Descending the ridge to Bearwallow Gap, an intersection with the **Whiteoak Flats/Hickey Branch Trail** is crossed. Currently there is no sign on this unmarked trail. There is a double white blaze on the tree in the path fork, however, and the junction is less than ¼ mile north from the Blackstack Cliffs sign. The footpath descends into North Carolina and reaches rough jeep USFS

Route 465, in about ¾ mile. The old road leads to rural route NC-1310, which intersects NC-212, in an estimated 6 miles. (See **Whiteoak Flats/Hickey Branch** entry.)

From the gnarled beech trees and rhododendron slicks of Bearwallow Gap, the Appalachian Trail skirts the Firescald Bald summit area, beneath more high white cliffs. Shortly, in the next gap, blue blazes of the **Phillips Hollow Trail** (including a weathered sign) are passed on the left. This route turns northwest from the summit to road Access 1 of the Greene Mountain section, a distance of about 3 miles.

Continuing north, the next major intersection is the **Round Knob Trail**. This junction has a sign to Round Knob, but currently pointing more to the white blazed route and listing a distance of 2 miles. The footpath (without blazes) down the Tennessee side of the ridge leads about ½ mile along the old roadbed to a parking turnaround for off-road users. There are barriers and hiker-only notices at the turnaround. A washboard of a road—and a roller coaster course in places—this route is used by hunters and off-road vehicles when open. It is easily followed on foot for an estimated 2.5 more miles to the picnic shelter/parking area and the system of hiker/horse trails at Round Knob.

The white blazes continue with the old road tracks northeastward. Officially closed to vehicle, horse and pack stock traffic, the old road once connected the Round Knob and Horse Creek Areas. The **Fork Ridge Trail** (also referred to as the Big Creek Trail in some guides to the area) descends southward to the Big Creek and Carmen areas of North Carolina and is met about one mile from the Round Knob turn. The Fork Ridge route is marked with a vertical metal sign and hiker only notices. The Jerry Cabin Shelter is located a few hundred yards further. From the shelter, it is about 2½ miles to the diversion of the **Horse Creek Trail**, which descends the old road on the Tennessee side of the mountain to the Horse Creek Recreation Area. The ridge crests in this area retain several brush meadows, balds and rocky points with good views. Also, about 200 yards before reaching the Horse Creek Road turn, the yellow blazes of the **Sarvis Cove Trail** turn left to descend the ridge.

Section 3:
Continuing Appalachian Trail: Horse Creek Trail Junction north to Devil's Fork Gap—About 6.5 miles.
Map for this segment is on page 189.

The Horse Creek Road turns diagonally from the white marked route to a gate below the summit area. A side trail leads to the Big Rock view of the Tennessee valleys to the north. The **Horse Creek Trail** is a multi-use route. It is wide and easily followed 4 miles to the pavement at the Horse Creek Recreation Area.

Continuing along the white marked trail, the route follows a rough jeep road through another area of brush meadows, the last for several miles. A less-traveled track turns left from the grassy field to a crude shed used by hunters and hikers. The **Squibb Creek Trail** begins its descent of Rich Mountain in this area. The Appalachian Trail turns generally southeastward from this butte (Big Rock 4,838 feet), and another nearby high point, the Big Butt. The route follows the wooded ridge line for about 3 miles to Flint Gap and trail intersection with the **Rocky Fork/Flint Creek Trail**.

As a point of interest, about midway between the Horse Creek turn and Flint Gap there are two grave stones in a small park like grove. The headstones mark the grave of William and David Shelton. These brothers were Union soldiers during the Civil War and were visiting their family's cabin near this spot when they and a lookout were killed by Confederates. All three were buried here, but the markers in the quiet forest note only the Shelton brothers graves, since the government purchased stones only for soldiers.

At Flint Gap the **Rocky Fork Trail** or **Flint Creek Trail** turns down a steep bank to the northeast, to a small creek in the ravine. In about ¼ mile the route widens along an old railroad bed and follows the bank of a large stream for about 4 easy miles to the Rocky Fork area. (See Rocky Fork Trail entry.)

The trail shelter for this area is reached in about ¾ mile from Flint Gap. From Flint Gap, the route heads nearly due south until it reaches Devils Fork Gap on NC-212, in about 3.5 miles of mostly gradual downhill grade.

There is developed parking beside NC-212. The continuing Appalachian Trail route to points north crosses the road and cattle pasture at Devils Fork Gap, but still leading south here.

Devil's Fork Access

This car access is on North Carolina 212/Tennessee 352. The large turnout/parking and prominent white trail blazes are 4.4 miles southwest from U.S. Highway 23 at the crossroads of Rocky Fork. The TN-352/U.S-23 junction is 10 miles from the new south Erwin exit of Interstate 181 (later to be I-26). There will be closer exits to Rocky Fork when the Interstate is completed.

Continuing southwest on NC-212 from the Appalachian Trail crossing,

NC-208 is 14.6 miles. Roads up Big Creek for the **Big Creek Trail** and Hickey Branch to the **Whiteoak Flats Trail** both turn right en route from winding, paved NC-212. Allen Gap is 5.8 miles north on NC-208. The highway becomes TN-70 at the gap and continues on to Greeneville, or to access points described in the Greene Mountain chapter.

Note Possible Route and Designation Changes:

Construction of Interstate 181/26 is proceeding to link Erwin to the North Carolina line. Exactly how this will effect the current routing of U.S. 23 is uncertain, although it should remain as it is, at least in the Rocky Fork area.

Rocky Fork Trail

Trail distance: 4 miles, one way.
Difficulty rating: Easy.
Horse/Mountain Bike Use.

The Rocky Fork Trail is an easy, graded route along an old railroad bed. Following the branching of Flint Creek westward, the designated horse trail is wide and clearly defined, although unmarked. It reaches the **Appalachian Trail** in 4 miles.

The trail head is reached by turning north from U.S. 23 at the first road before the junction of TN-352. (Note that these roads are only a couple hundred yards apart.) This point is 10 miles from the current south Erwin exit of Interstate 181 (there will be closer exits when the current construction is completed). There is a "Rocky Fork Creek" sign. The newly paved road reaches a turnout/parking on the left in one mile. There is a large wooden sign and parking for 2 or 3 cars near the gate.

This walk begins along the right bank of the large creek. It is a wide, rushing stream for about the first mile, with deep rapids and low falls. There is a shaky bridge after the first fork, and the route crosses to the left bank along the main track. After the stream flow is reduced by branches, there are several fords and smaller falls in the 30 foot range. Continue along the main branch, generally to the west; logging roads intersect along the route.

At 3½ to 4 miles from the start, the route is through a narrow ravine, and the creek flow is only about one foot wide. At the end of this hollow, the trail switches back to the south and climbs steeply up the ridge for ¼ mile to Flint Gap and the junction with the **Appalachian Trail**.

Icicles coat the creek side along Flint Creek on the Rocky Fork Trail.

South/East Bald Mountains Area

Trails From North Carolina 212 and 208
Big Creek, Fork Ridge, Whiteoak Flats/Hickey Branch, Pounding
Mill Trails and Appalachian Trail Connections in the Pisgah
National Forest
Map for this area is on page 189.

Trails in this area are along the southeastern slopes of the Bald Mountains in the Pisgah National Forest of North Carolina. Public Access points are not as well marked, and there are no developed campgrounds as is the case on the Tennessee side of this range. However, the scenery of small farms and coves set against the mountains makes the drive very rewarding. The paths on this side of the mountain are used less than those of the north/west slopes (Horse Creek/Greene Mountain areas), but many of the trails connect via the Appalachian Trail along the summit.

Appalachian Trail hiker passes through beds of fringed phacelia.

ails in this section are from country lanes turning from North Carolina or 208. (Also, see Access points for Devil's Fork, Horse Creek and Greene Mountain areas.)

NC-212 is reached by turning from U.S. 23 at Rocky Fork, south of Erwin, onto Tennessee 352. At 4.4 miles the state line is crossed. The Appalachian Trail crossing is just beyond the border sign, and the paved road changes route numbers to NC-212 at this point. Rural route NC-1312 is marked with a small vertical metal post and turns right at 7.7 miles from U.S 23, at the Carmen Church of God. Rural NC-1310 is 12.0 miles from Rocky Fork, just before reaching Cutshalls Grocery.

Landmarks for general orientation are the fire tower and communications installations atop Camp Creek Bald. They are visible all along the valley and at clearings on the ridges. These make good reference points for compass reading.

Big Creek Trail
Trail distance: 3 miles, one way, estimated.
Difficulty rating: Easy.
Horse/Mountain Bike Use.

The Big Creek Trail is a beautiful, easy, creek-side walk of an estimated 3 miles. Most of the route could be an excellent horse trail as well as hiker path, since there are no use restrictions posted. There are no signs or trail markings, and few landmarks.

The trail head is reached by turning from NC-212 at 7.7 miles from U.S. Highway 23, or 11.5 miles from the NC-208 junction. Turn beside the Carmen Church of God onto paved Route 1312 (where there is a small vertical metal marker). Drive 2.4 miles along this lane, which turns to gravel en route, and turn left at wooden sign noting U.S. Forest Service Route 111. The road crosses a low water, concrete ford at this point, and a Pisgah National Forest boundary sign is reached in about ¼ mile. Continue along a good gravel road about one mile, then cross two concrete, low water bridges. Park just beyond second bridge or walk from first ford.

Just across the last bridge, there is a clearing/turnaround. In this small clearing a metal Forest Service sign notes the **Fork Ridge Trail** head. It has a hiker-only notice.

The Big Creek Trail continues straight along the gravel lane, and the first stream ford is just ahead. The creek is several yards across, shallow and tumbling. From the first crossing (on stepping stones) the route is no longer maintained, but the old road bed is still fairly clear. It probably gets some horse traffic, but the day I was up it, in early spring, there was little sign of any type of recent use. The route narrows with each stream crossing, and for the first couple of miles, it is a clear, single-file path with a very slight grade. The direction of travel is generally to the northeast through a long narrow hollow, with the higher gaps on the ridge lines appearing close (although one never seems to get there).

At around 2 miles the path makes a detour from the old logging route, becoming less defined and steeper. Old sawdust mounds are reached at about 3 miles. The trail from this point can still be made out intermittently, but essentially it has been reclaimed by the regrowth forest. In winter it may be possible to continue along this route to the crest and connections with the Appalachian Trail and other trails. It would, however, be difficult going, and is not recommended in the growing season when tracks are obscured.

Hikers on the Appalachian Trail take a break atop the White Rocks overlook on the Tennessee/North Carolina border.

In late April this route has good displays of wild flowers, including (at least three) trillium varieties, wild geranium, and patches of dwarf iris. A pleasant stroll.

Fork Ridge Trail
Trail distance: 2.5 miles, approximate, one way.
Difficulty rating: Difficult.
Appalachian Trail connector.

This hiker-only footpath is listed primarily as a connector to the

palachian Trail. The route intersects the white blazed route on the summit near the Jerry Cabin Shelter. It is recommended for hardier souls who don't mind some climbing and occasional obstructions to challenge them.

This route is also referred to as the Big Creek Trail in some area guidebooks, since this is where it terminates when followed from the summit. There are faded yellow trail blazes, and the route can be primitive, especially late in the growing season. (For the creek trail head see the **Big Creek Trail**, above.)

This trail intersects the Appalachian Trail in the summit area, less than ¼ mile south of the Jerry Cabin Shelter. There is a vertical metal sign and hiker-only notices at the junction.

Whiteoak Flats/Hickey Branch Trail
Trail distance: Approximately 4 miles, one way.
Difficulty rating: Easy to moderate.
Appalachian Trail connector.
Horse/Mountain Bike Use.

Older maps as well as recent trail guides show the **Whiteoak Flats Trail** making connections with several area trails along the southeastern slopes of the bald mountains. These include the **Pounding Mill** and **Appalachian Trails**, just below Camp Creek Bald on its western end, and connections with the Big Creek Trails on its eastern end. However, due to recent logging operations and rapid growth of thickets and new forest, I can only vouch for the route listed below. Probable access points for the other connections are noted.

Road Access: Turn from NC-212 onto gravel road NC-1310, 12 miles from U.S. 23, or 7.3 miles from NC-208, at 0.2 mile from Cutshalls Grocery. The Pisgah National Forest boundary sign is passed at 1.2 miles, where the road becomes USFS-495. This single track road is along tumbling Hickey Branch (listed as "Hickory Branch" on some maps). At 2.7 miles from NC-212, take the right fork of the lane; the newer, left fork travels another ½ mile to a large parking/turnaround, the head of an unmarked trail, and a newly constructed logging road with a closed gate. I've walked the gravel surface logging road for about 3 miles, around the ridge sides to the slopes of Camp Creek Bald, but did not encounter the other trails. Perhaps they were just around the next bend, or were obliterated, or were located along the above mentioned unmarked path (this is the most probable).

Taking the right fork of the road, as above, most vehicles can drive the rough lane for another 1.7 miles before parking in one of the narrow turnouts.

There are no signs or use restriction notices. Small off-road vehicles or horses can continue for another 3 or 3½ miles on the eroded jeep track. On foot, the route is easy to follow and there are few really steep sections, although it climbs steadily. At about ¾ mile from the above mentioned parking, an area of intersecting jeep tracks is encountered. The second fork to the right is probably the old route to the Big Creek Area. This junction can be identified by an old rock wall or foundation in the fork. The route up the mountain is the left branch.

Switchbacks lead up the ridges toward the summit, and there are good views en route. At about 3½ miles from the parking, a small gap is reached on the west shoulder of the ridge. In another 100 feet a less used route turns in the direction of Camp Creek bald, rather than climb the hill. Here the main track narrows and loops on upward for a short distance before it disappears into the brush and briars and other rarely used routes fanning out from the hilltop. The continuing path to the crest was once an old jeep road, but it is now partly obstructed with briars, dead falls and rhododendron thickets.

Old fence frames western North Carolina mountains.

It is definitely a footpath only for the remaining ½ to ¾ mile to Bearwallow Gap and the junction with the **Appalachian Trail** and is currently rated moderate.

This final link is clear enough and well defined now, but without maintenance to trim back the dense rhododendron, it will probably disappear in a few more seasons.

The junction with the Appalachian Trail is on the summit in a grove of gnarled beech trees. The rocky summit of Firescald Bald is visible to the east. Turning west on the white marked path, the wooden sign to Blackstack Cliffs is less than ¼ mile. Another ¼ mile leads to the White Rocks overlook path, and this turn is also marked with a wooden sign nailed to a tree. There are dramatic 180 degree views from these white cliffs.

Pounding Mill Trail

Trail distance: 6 miles, one way, approximate.
Difficulty rating: Difficult.

The trail head for the Pounding Mill Trail is on the east side of NC-208 at 2.1 miles from the Allen Gap crossing of the Appalachian Trail. There is a small vertical metal marker for the route, along with hiker-only notices. Turnout/parking is provided on the west side of the highway.

The Forest Service has given this trail a ''Most Difficult'' rating. It is recommended for those seeking a challenge or a more wilderness-like experience than can be found on the more popular routes. It makes connections with the Appalachian Trail, via the Whiteoak Flats Trail, and (on recent maps) other primitive routes in the Little Laurel and Camp Creek Bald.

Appalachian Trail

Devil's Fork Gap, north to Chestoa

Segment 1: Devil's Fork Gap to Sam's Gap
Trail segment distance: 7.8 miles, one way.
Difficulty rating: Moderate.

Maps for this segment are on pages 189 and 190.

The first link in this segment, which stretches from Devil's Fork Gap to U.S. 23 at Sam's Gap, is 7.8 miles. Much of the distance is over private lands, although the Forest Service has acquired strips along the crest for the Appalachian Trail right-of-way. This segment begins by crossing a fence stile from Route 212/352 after which it passes through a pasture and small wood, then down through a couple of bottom land farms along Boone Cove Road. This narrow lane can be used as a car access, but there is little parking. The trail crosses the road at 1.3 miles from the Boone Cove/TN 352 junction at the Sweetwater Church. From this rural lane the trail climbs back to high forest, with most of the distance lying along ridges. Occasional alpine meadows present views of small farms below Rice and Sam's Gaps. The trail route continues along the crests of the Bald Mountains, straddling the imaginary line that divides Tennessee and North Carolina. There are long, moderate climbs, mostly graded by switchbacks. This trail link may receive considerable traffic by hunters with their dogs during hunting season, but normally it is not one of the more popular segments of the footpath. There are no developed connecting trails in the segment, although there is some trail bike use from old logging roads. Weed and stinging nettle growth may be heavy during summer under the cutover woods.

Attractions included views from high pastures (and from high knobs, although these are screened by trees of surrounding communities) and beds of wildflowers (such as spring beauties and fringed phacelia), also prolific under the budding maples and tulip poplars in early spring).

Access 1:
Devil's Fork Gap on NC 212/TN 352 is 4.4 miles from U.S. 23 at Rocky Fork.

Access 2:

Rice Gap is 6 miles from U.S. 23 along the secondary road turning beside Rice's Store at Flag Pond. This access may be difficult, since the old road that once crossed the mountain has been closed. Currently it is little more than a jeep rut. Rice Gap may be approached from the North Carolina side via NC-1341, but this approach is all but abandoned, too.

Access 3:

Sam's Gap is on U.S. 23 at the North Carolina/Tennessee border. Note that this point may be altered slightly due to Interstate Highway construction in this area. Interstate 181, currently being built, is to terminate at the state line, but eventually Interstate 26 is to connect with I-181 at this point, and the route designation changed to I-26.

Segment 2: Sam's Gap, on U.S. 23, to Spivey Gap, at U.S. 19W.
Trail segment distance: 12.2 miles, one way.
Difficulty rating: Moderate, but with strenuous grades.

Maps for this segment are on pages 189 and 190.

There are long climbs from either end of this segment, but the link presents outstanding views from the true Appalachian Bald atop Big Bald Mountain, which rises to 5,516 feet. The section from Street Gap to the bald has beautiful displays of fringed phacelia, trillium and trout lilies in early May, appearing as a solid carpet of wildflowers through the woods. Most of this section is through dense forest, but between Sam's and Street Gaps there are beautiful open pastures that still appear much as the crests of this whole range appeared 80-100 years ago.

Popular round trip day hikes to Big Bald Mountain begin at either Street or Sam's Gap. The distance is for 8 miles from the former, 12 from the latter.

Just below the bald area, a secondary trail with blue painted blazes circles the southern rim of the summit, and a closed gravel road leads to the ski/second home resort of Wolf Laurel. Otherwise there are no secondary trails in this segment open to hikers. The Paul Fink Trail has disappeared into a maze of storm downed trees; it once turned from the Big Stamp, bald saddle area (just north from the summit by the white blazes) to descend the Tennessee slopes.

Intermittent bald areas line about one mile of the path; these stretch from each side of Big Bald. The Appalachian Trail Shelter is reached after entering birch woods north of the balds. For those seeking greater thrills, the High

Rock area (which is about 1 to 1.5 miles from the U.S. 19-W end of the section) offers an orange marked route for those interested in rock climbing, rapelling, and testing other survival skills. The white marked path offers challenge enough, with a steep grade through dark hemlock, pine and rhododendron, and safety cables to help with slippery footing along the rocks.

Street Gap Access

Traveling south on U.S. 23, turn left onto Higgins Creek Road, just beyond the community of Flag Pond, Tennessee. The turn has a sign for Higgins Creek Chapel. After passing under I-181 turn right onto a narrow lane at 1.8 miles from U.S. 23. This road can be traveled in good weather by cars with above average traction. The road has a sign noting it as Right Fork Higgins Creek, and it is followed to the summit, where white trail blazes are visible. This gap may be approached from the North Carolina side by the somewhat steeper Puncheon Fork Road.

Also, note that Interstate Highway construction in the area may alter some of these distances or road conditions.

Street Gap is two miles by trail from Sam's Gap, or about four from Big Bald Mountain.

U.S. Highway 19-W Access: Near Spivey Gap, for Appalachian, Devils Creek and Lost Cove/Joe Lewis Trails.

The Appalachian Trail crossing of U.S. 19-W is well marked with a sign and a large turnout/parking area. The junction is 1.3 miles inside North Carolina, before the eastern slope from the gap. The white blazed trail may also be intersected by turning up USFS-278 (north from highway), located 0.3 mile back toward Tennessee. The Appalachian Trail crosses the gravel lane at 1.5 miles from U.S. 19-W, at the turn of USFS-5506. The Earnestville junction of U.S. 23/U.S.19-W and I-181 are around 8 miles away by very twisting blacktop, but waterfalls along Spivey Creek are passed en route. Burnsville is the nearest town on the North Carolina side.

In July the area near this trail head has prolific areas of blooming white rhododendron.

Two other nearby trails, the Lost Cove/Joe Lewis Fields and Devil's Creek/Bearwoods Trails, offer good day hikes in the Flattop Mountain and Lost Cove areas. The trail head for the **Devil's Creek/Bear Woods Trail** is reached by turning north onto USFS-278 (the Flat Top Mountain Road), located 0.3 mile toward the Tennessee line from the Appalachian Trail crossing of U.S. 19-W. At 1.5 miles, USFS-5506 (a closed timber road) turns left; the Appalachian Trail also crosses here, as noted above. This is the head of the Devil's Creek Trail.

Continue along Route 278 for around 3 to 4 miles more miles (high ground clearance is required for vehicles beyond the USFS-5506 junction) to where USFS-5505 (another closed timber road) turns left, or approach it from the other end. (See Lost Cove entry.) This is the **Lost Cove Trail** head.

Lost Cove/Joe Lewis Fields Trail
Trail distance: 2 miles, one way to junction of Devil's Creek Trail.
Difficulty rating: Mostly moderate, with steep sections.

The Lost Cove Trail (also called Joe Lewis Fields Trail) is trail number 196 of the Pisgah National Forest, Toecane Ranger District. The trail is heavily used during hunting season, is well defined, and easily followed through old fields and cutover forest. There are dramatic views of the Nolichuckey River Gorge and the land locked village of Lost Cove (which is private property) from the Flattop Mountain Ridge.

Developed during construction of the railroad through the Nolichuckey River gorge in the early part of the century, the Lost Cove Community was once complete with a school, church, grist mill and several small homes. Its residents remained until around the 1950's, making their living by subsistence farming and logging. Ironically, the railroad which caused its founding also helped bring the community's demise by suspending passenger service after World War II. Many of the old homes and barns stand as their owners left them, but the area is on private property.

This walk can be combined with the Devil's Creek Trail and USFS-278 for a circuit walk of approximately 9-10 miles.

To reach the trail head: Drive 4.4 miles east on U.S. 19-W from the Appalachian Trail crossing, near Spivey Gap; turn left onto rural NC-1415 (numbers are on the stop sign post); drive 1.3 miles to 3 way fork in the road; and take left branch onto USFS-278. The middle prong of this fork is used as a horse and trail bike route to the Nolichuckey River, and is a moderately rated walk in the 3-4 mile range. Other hiker trails also turn from graveled USFS-278. These closed timber roads lead to clear cuts near or overlooking the river gorge. At 3.4 miles from U.S. 19-W, a hiker-only notice marks a path and closed road turning up a steep slope to planted fields atop the ridge. This is the head of the Lost Cove/Joe Lewis Trail. USFS-278 becomes impassable except for high ground clearance vehicles at this point, although it continues for 3-4 miles to the Devil's Creek Trail head and to U.S. 19-W. There is good turnout parking at the trail head.

The trail climbs to the top of the ridge. The old Joe Lewis fields are seeded to grass meadows atop the high knobs of Flattop Mountain. From the grassy summit there are excellent 360 degree panoramas of the surrounding mountainscape, and short side paths lead to better views into the river gorge. The continuing footpath crosses the crest in the swag toward the west (northwest from entering the field, in the small gap between the knobs). There is a vertical metal trail marker and an old road bed turning down along the ridge.

The path leads down the ridge by a series of switch backs along an old road bed. Most of the grades are moderate, but there are steep and rocky sections. The forest is regrowth hardwoods, with occasional old hemlocks,

A day hiker walks along the Joe Lewis Fields overlooking the Lost Cove and Nolichuckey River areas.

maples and poplars. At two spots along the hillside, underground streams can be heard rushing beneath the rocks and boulders. There are infrequent, faded white paint blazes along the well defined trail. All views are screened by the forest below the crest.

At a point at least 2 miles below the summit, clear new blazes are painted on two trees a few feet apart. There is a distinct "B" carved into the bark of the first tree. The trail leading between the trees and turning westward is less distinct; it leads to the Devil's Creek/Bearwoods Trail. There are painted blazes, but initially the route can be hard to follow even in early summer.

The old road continues downhill by switchbacks. In the western tip of the next one, an old fire or logging road can be spotted turning west along the ridge. Although it is unmarked, it is frequently used, and it also leads to the junction of the Devil's Creek/Bearwoods Trail. Property and no tress-passing notices of Lost Cove are met along the main track in about another mile. A good graded track, with faint white blazes continues eastward from this junction with faint paint blazes going away from the lane into the private lands.

Devil's Creek/Bear Woods Trail
Trail distance: 3 miles, one way, estimated.
Difficulty rating: Easy, west end—moderate to difficult, east end.

Also called the Bear Woods Trail, this is Pisgah National Forest trail number 188. (See access points for Appalachian Trail and Lost Cove Trail.) It is clear and maintained. The area traversed is below Flattop Mountain's north flank. The first 1.5 miles (estimated) are along closed timber road USFS-5506, and there are views from clear cuts of the river gorge and the Unaka and Roan Mountain areas to the northeast. The road then reaches planted wildlife meadows and a closed gate. At this point white blazes mark the intersection of paths from the Lost Cove Trail.

The small blazed path continues northeast along the ridge side through low hanging rhododendron and evergreens, with small stream crossings. The wide, graded path of the Joe Lewis Fields Trail is met in about 1½ miles.

Segment 3: Continuing south to north

Map for this segment is on page 190.

Spivey Gap to Chestoa/Nolichuckey River Access near Erwin.
Trail segment distance: 10.2 miles, one way.
Difficulty rating: Moderate from south to north, but due to long strenuous climbs from the other end, it is rated difficult north to south. It is steep and can be slippery in either direction.

From steep cliffs near the northern end of walk, this section offers good views of the deep canyon of the Nolichuckey River. The route between is through Pisgah and Cherokee National Forest lands, with several old timber roads and primitive trails that turn toward the old Lost Cove Community (mentioned in the Lost Cove and Devil's Creek entries). A route with views outside the private property boundaries is crossed at about 1.5 miles from U.S. 19-W, see Devil's Creek entry.

The No Business Knob shelter is just beyond the midway point of the segment and the beginning of a long descent to the Unaka Springs Community on the Nolichuckey River. The trail then crosses the river by a single lane concrete bridge (which is to be replaced, resulting in some re-routing); then it goes up the east bank of the river by a gravel road.

Chestoa Access:

There is a Forest Service sign on U.S. 23 near the I-181 south Erwin exit directing travelers to the Chestoa Recreation Area. The trail turns from the gravel lane toward Curley Maple Gap, near the road's dead end and the white water rafting headquarters of Nolichuckey Expeditions. This company and another one called Cherokee Adventures offer trips through the gorge which range from breathtaking to serene. The continuation of the Appalachian Trail is in the following Unaka Mountain section.

Map for this area is on page 190.

Tracks of wildlife revealed by an early winter snow storm.

Unaka Mountain Area

Including Rock Creek Falls, Red Fork Falls, Beauty Spot and Appalachian Trail.

Map for this area is on page 191.

The Unaka Mountain area offers attractions that range from tumbling creeks with waterfalls to outstanding high vistas. It is one of the most scenic areas of the Cherokee and Pisgah National Forest. In addition to the Appalachian Trail, there are numerous other developed and primitive paths, as well as the newly designated Unaka Mountain Wilderness Area.

How to Get There

Approaches to the area are listed from Interstate 181, Exits 23 and 19. **Note possible Exit number changes, and highway number changes, with the completion of the Interstate now under construction to the North Carolina border.** The Interstate is eventually to be redesignated I-26.

Route 1: From the Unicoi Community Exit (Currently I-181/Exit 23).

The current I-181/ Exit 23 sign notes Route 173/Unicoi Road at the ramp. Follow Route 173 east, join U.S. 19-W/U.S. 23 south briefly, and at the Unicoi crossroads continue on Route 173/TN 107 east toward Buladean, North Carolina. The Limestone Cove Recreation Area is passed on the left at 3.6 miles. The **Rocky Branch Trail** begins on the opposite side of the highway and leads to intersections with the **Limestone Cove** and **Stamping Ground Ridge Trails**. At the next country store, Route 173 turns northeast to connect with U.S. 19-E between Hampton and Roan Mountain. Continue on TN-107 east, toward Iron Mountain Gap.

At 7.4 miles from the Unicoi crossroads, Red Fork Creek (marked by a small sign) is crossed. The next gravel road turning right (near the D.O.T. 13 milepost) at ½ mile is Forest Service Unaka Mountain Road, note it for access points along the crest of the mountain. The road travels generally westward to **Red Fork Falls, Unaka Mountain Recreation Area Trails, Beauty Spot** and **Appalachian Trail** access points; then it intersects Tennessee 395 atop the mountain at Indian Grave Gap. Route 395 descends the mountain, passing the Rock Creek Recreation Area, to connect with Route 2 coming up the same road from Erwin.

Appalachian Trail/Iron Mountain Gap Access

Drive to the top of the mountain on TN-107. The Appalachian Trail crossing at Iron Mountain Gap is 2.6 miles beyond the westward turn of Unaka Mountain Road, or 10.7 miles from the U.S. 23 junction at the Unicoi Community. There is a sign at the gap, and ample parking. Going south, the trail winds up Iron Mountain to Little Bald Knob, then down to Cherry Gap, finally crossing to Unaka Mountain. North from this access leads to Hughes Gap and points in the Roan Mountain segment. At Iron Mountain Gap, Tennessee 107 becomes North Carolina 226, which continues east.

Route 2: From Erwin I-181/Exit 19.
Appalachian Trail/Indian Grave Gap Access

This exit from Interstate 181 is noted with a sign for Main Street, and the golden arches of the fast food strip can be seen. Note possible exit number changes when the Interstate is finally completed, and the corridor becomes I-26. Turn toward the McDonald's and Hardee's signs (which probably will not change). About a block beyond these restaurants, Route 395 turns left from the combined TN 107/U.S. 23 main drag. There is a sign and traffic light at the intersection.

The turn into the Rock Creek Recreation Area is 3.2 miles on the left. The **Appalachian Trail** crosses at the crest, 6.3 miles from the traffic light. There are no signs, but the white trail blazes can be spotted, and there is good parking. This is Indian Grave Gap, and it is on the state line. The main road continues to Poplar, North Carolina. The rough gravel lane turning left is the Unaka Mountain Road, and a right turn for Beauty Spot is about 2 miles east along it.

Map for this area is on page 190.

Red Fork Falls and Trail

Red Fork Falls are a short walk from the graveled Unaka Mountain Road. There are no signs along the roadway, however, and spotting the path may be difficult. To locate the trail, note the mileage at the turn from Route 107. There is a small turnout on the right shoulder of the lane at 1.2 miles. There is a faded white ring around a tree at this point, and a wide swath angles toward the creek.

There are no trail blazes. To reach the falls, walk 175 yards along the track to the first fork of the creek, ford it and the second fork (about 100 feet ahead). Both branches of the stream are only inches deep, and there are stepping stones for crossing. Follow the path downstream, along the left bank; the top of the falls are reached in ¼ mile or less. From the top of the cascades, the trail is nearly vertical, but there are natural handholds and steps in the rocks. The descent is only slightly more difficult than a ladder or steep stairs, although it is slippery and treacherous.

Be careful! A young man recently fell from the top of the falls and was killed.

From the base of the main falls, smaller, less dramatic cascades continue down the ravine for another 100 yards, more or less, making a sharp bend and ending in quiet pools. The main falls are in the 80 foot range and carry enough water to be impressive. The branch can be followed downstream by primitive fishing paths to its crossing of Route 107. These continuing paths are ill defined and in the difficult range, with detours around thickets and along the ridge.

Rock Creek Falls and Trail

Trail distance: 2.5 miles, estimated, one way.
Difficulty rating: Moderate, due to several stream crossings.
Connecting paths: Rattlesnake Ridge Trail, and Appalachian Trail via a difficult, primitive path; adding one mile to the distance.

The trail to Rock Creek Falls begins at the end of the paved road through the Rock Creek Recreation Area campground. There is parking at the rest rooms and picnic area. The road into the recreation area from Route 395 may be closed in winter, placing the trail head about ½ mile away, at the end of the pavement.

There are no signs at the start of the walk, but the route is easily found since it is the old road bed continuing near the right bank of the steam. The

Rock Creek waterfalls tumble from the highlands on the Rock Creek Trail.

turn of the **Rattlesnake Ridge Trail** to Unaka Mountain is noted with a new sign, within 100 yards of the pavement's end.

The Rock Creek Trail is a wide, well defined, aging road bed which, for most of the distance to the two waterfalls, would fall within the easy stroll category, except for the stream crossings which can be treacherous after rains. There are a couple of foot logs, but mostly it is either wade across or jump from rock to rock. There are occasional metal diamond blazes that have survived the vandals.

The walk is a pleasant one through regrowth forest of mixed Appalachian Hardwoods. A tall understory of Rhododendron Maximum fills the woods with white blossoms in early July. The tumbling stream has numerous small cascades; the first falls are approximately 2 miles from the campground. They are viewed from up the ridge as the trail climbs above them. Slippery side paths descend to the pool below. The first falls is in the 40 foot range.

Continuing upstream by the old road, the second and higher falls is about another ½ mile. At the last stream crossing before reaching the second falls, look for a double metal blaze marking a small fork of the trail. This is the beginning of a primitive, difficult route to above the falls, with connections to the Unaka Mountain Road and the **Appalachian Trail** atop the mountain.

The second falls are 70 feet high, in two steps, and drop into an amphitheater like basin formed by the surrounding cliffs.

The continuing route is recommended only for the more agile explorer types, since a small amount of rock climbing is required up the cliffs, and the trail is ill defined on up the mountain. To reach the top of the mountain, the ravine may be scaled along the path mention above, or by picking out the path along the east side of the falls. Atop the rock walls there are rhododendron thickets to scrape through when going back to the creek. With luck, yellow painted blazes will be spotted on trees as the stream begins to feather out. The path is marked only in one direction, however, and could be missed.

Nearing the summit, a blue blazed water trail for the **Appalachian Trail** will be encountered near the road, if all goes well. Should the path be lost, just head for the crest, traveling south, and the gravel road will soon be intersected. The road and the top of the falls are no more than one mile apart.

Finding the route from the top could be more difficult. Traveling on the gravel lane east from the Beauty Spot turn, a blue blazed water trail from the **Appalachian Trail** crosses the road in the first sag, at 1.5 miles. Follow the blazes to the spring; then converging spring branches down to the main creek and the falls cliffs.

Red Fork Falls, a short walk from Unaka Mountain Road.

Rattlesnake Ridge Trail
Trail distance: 4 miles, one way, estimated.
Difficulty rating: Moderate.

The Rattlesnake Ridge Trail is a well defined footpath leading from the Rock Creek Recreation Area campground through the recently designated Unaka Mountain Wilderness Area, and terminating at the Unaka Mountain Scenic Area atop the mountain.

At the bottom of the mountain, the route turns from the Rock Creek Trail a few yards from the end of the pavement at the campground. Initially the route heads northeastward in a marshy area, then runs along an old road to Dick Creek Gap, reached in about one mile. At the gap there is a clearing/turnaround for off-road vehicles. The old road, continuing toward the northeast, is probably USFS-307 leading to TN-107 west of the Limestone Cove Recreation Area. The Rattlesnake Ridge Trail turns right, generally toward the south, and goes up the ridge from the clearing. There is a Unaka Mountain Wilderness sign within 100 yards. The hiker-only route up the ridge is by a moderately graded track (probably an old road) and reaches the summit and Unaka Mountain Road in another three miles, conservatively estimated.

Rocky Branch,
Limestone Cove
and Stamping Ground Ridge Trails

These horse routes intersect on Stamping Ground Ridge to connect the Unaka Recreation Area to points on Route 107, at Limestone Cove Campground and the community of the same name at the 173/107 crossroads. The **Rocky Branch Trail** head is at the Recreation area; the **Limestone Cove Trail** is further east on the highway. These two are above average in difficulty, with steep and marshy sections, but are fairly easy to follow since they are used by weekend horse enthusiasts and some off-road vehicles. The only signs or blazes are at the trail heads. The routes are about 4 miles long and intersect the **Stamping Ground Ridge** route on the ridge of that name.

The routes atop the mountain can be found by driving west along the Unaka Mountain Road for 6 miles. There are broken concrete picnic tables on this overlook/trail head. The rough roads and their routes down the mountain to the Limestone Cove area can be traced from this clear view point.

A winter view from Beauty Spot, looking west, along the Appalachian Trail.

Appalachian Trail

North from Chestoa to Iron Mountain Gap

Segment 1: Chestoa/Nolichuckey River to Indian Grave Gap/TN-395.
Trail distance: Approximately 8.5 miles, one way.
Difficulty rating: Difficult, due to long steep climb from the Nolichuckey River Gorge.

Map for this segment is on page 190.

This segment of the Appalachian Trail begins at the Chestoa picnic area near the south Erwin Exit of I-181. There is a Forest Service sign on U.S. 23 pointing to the recreation area. White trail blazes currently lead along the gravel road on the east side of the river, but due to road construction and trail rerouting to the ridges, some looking around for the blazes could be required and the mileage could be increased.

After leaving the river the route begins a 3½ to 4 mile climb, gaining nearly 1,500 feet en route. Along the way there are several small stream crossings and a few screen views. There are intersecting paths at the Curley Maple Shelter atop the mountain; these are old logging roads that can be explored. One old lane turning to the southwest makes a long loop around the point of the mountain to Ephraim Place; then it turns back to the northeast (marked by off-road vehicle tracks) to emerge at Indian Grave Gap at the junctions of the Appalachian Trail/TN 395/Unaka Mountain Road on the summit.

Following the white blazes north from the shelter, the remaining four miles to the paved road crossing at Indian Grave Gap is fairly easy. En route, short-cuts (used mostly by hunters) down to TN-395 can also be spotted.

Segment 2: Indian Grave Gap north to Iron Mountain Gap.
Beauty Spot and Unaka Mountain crossed en route.
Trail distance: 10.7 miles, one way.
Difficulty rating: Easy to Moderate.

Map for this segment is on page 191.

The Appalachian Trail crosses Indian Grave Gap 6.3 miles south of Erwin on TN-395. There is paved turnout parking and an unpaved Forest Service Road crossing in the gap. The paved road continues to Poplar, North Carolina.

The western branch of the Forest Service road is Route 132, which winds along the south side of the summit for about 2 miles to Ephraim Place. Old forest roads may be explored from there on foot.

The unpaved road turning eastward up the mountain shoulder is Unaka Mountain Road (USFS-230). The Appalachian Trail travels roughly parallel to this single track gravel road for several miles, and there are access points along the way.

North of TN-395, the white marked trail enters the forest through an arching laurel hallway to begin ascent of the mountain. The climb is gradual but steady, and passes through Appalachian Hardwoods. In about one mile the trail crosses the gravel forest service road, also ascending the mountain.

By car this point is 0.9 mile from the TN-395 junction.

The trail returns to the solitude of the forest and continues the slow climb of the ridge for another mile (more or less), then enters the meadows below Beauty Spot. Beauty Spot is 4,437 feet up, and is a typical Southern Appalachian Bald. It commands outstanding views of about 180 degrees, toward the west. There are long open fields of grass, ferns and brush, but much of the surrounding area is forested, which limits the arc toward the northeast. These fields are rimmed with blueberry bushes that are loaded with fruit in August.

Beauty Spot is reached by car by turning right at two miles from TN-395. This loop road leads to a parking area about 100 yards below the crest and trail crossing.

From the high point of Beauty Spot, the Appalachian Trail follows a gently meandering course within a few hundred yards of the gravel road for the next 2-3 miles. There are occasional views, slight grades, and open, fenced pastures between the high point and Beauty Spot Gap.

Traveling along the road from the Beauty Spot turn: A secondary water trail with blue blazes crosses the lane at 1.5 miles (see the **Rock Creek Trail** entry for route down the mountain here). A left turn into the Unaka Mountain Scenic Area (connecting with the **Rattlesnake Ridge Trail**) is 3 miles; Unaka Mountain Recreation Area, with its broken picnic tables and **Stamping Ground Ridge Trail** is another 1.3 miles; from there it is on to Red Fork Falls and Route 107. The total road mileage from TN-395 to TN-107 is approximately 12.5 miles.

Continuing the walk: As the road begins a series of switchbacks, climbing the mountain from Beauty Spot Gap (also called Deep Gap), the footpath begins the climb of Unaka mountain. This section has limited views from partially open meadows, but the peak (at 5,180 feet) is in an evergreen woods. The remaining 5.5 miles to Iron Mountain Gap is up and down ridges and through mature forest away from the road. Landmarks passed after the pinnacle include Low Gap, the Cherry Gap Shelter and Little Bald Knob.

Iron Mountain Gap north to Hughes Gap
Trail segment distance: 8.1 miles, one way.
Difficulty rating: Moderate to difficult, long climbs.

Maps for this segment are on pages 191 and 192.

This section of the Appalachian Trail is along the crest of the Iron Mountains; it follows the state lines and connects the Unaka and Roan Mountain segments. Traveling south to north, the initial couple of miles is flanked by private holdings of Christmas tree farms, old orchards, and heavily cut over wood lots. There are good views from these open areas. After returning to the forest there is considerable climbing. The Clyde Smith Shelter is reached in about 6 miles.

The main attractions of this segment are the dramatic cliffs and expansive views of Little Rock Knob, about 1.5 miles from the north end of this segment. Much of the rocky peak is wooded, but the overhanging cliffs offer a good 180 degree sweep. Directly below on the north slope is Tiger Creek/Roaring Creek Road, which loops past Ripshin Lake to emerge on U.S.19-E on each end. Bakersville, and (if it is clear) Spruce Pine can be spotted to the south. From the cliffs there is a long decline, and the route crosses a couple of small knolls and gaps before reaching the road at Hughes Gap.

Ascending Little Rock Knob from the Hughes Gap side is a torcherous climb (traveling north to south). I once met a group on this trail who described themselves as ''Slack Packers''; they were struggling up the ridge without even a water bottle between the three of them, speculating that the climb was surely longer than the offical 1.3 miles.

''This may be one of the famous A.T. IT's,'' said one of the hikers. ''It doesn't matter how long you climb, or how close IT looks, IT's always just a little farther.''

How to Get There

To reach this section by road, see the Roan Mountain segment for Hughes Gap, or the Unaka Mountain Chapter for the Iron Mountain Gap access. A little used access from Tiger Creek Road reaches Greasy Creek Gap about the middle of the section.

Tiger Creek Access:

Traveling east on U.S. 19-E from Hampton, Tiger Creek Road turns right ½ mile beyond the TN-173 junction (connecting with TN-107 at Limestone Cove). There is a small green street sign for Tiger Creek Road. Turn right at 5.4 miles onto a gravel road.

This lane is used as a driveway for a couple of houses, but at 0.1 mile Forest Service Route 4331 turns right. There is an orange gate across it, which is open in hunting season. The road can be driven by most vehicles. It winds for two miles to a recently clear cut area near the gap.

Park at the turnaround and begin walking along the path between red and yellow "Foot travel only" notices. This is a closed timber road with earth mound barriers. Follow the path, nearly due west, until you cross a blue blazed, secondary trail in about ¾ mile. The white blazed trail is approximately 300 yards farther along, near the crest of the ridge. The Appalachian Trail has recently been rerouted away from the rutted road atop the summit, but it may appear that there are dual routes, since much of the black paint used to cover the white blazes has weathered away.

Tiger Creek Road continues beyond the above turn to return to U.S. 19-E via Roaring Creek Road, passing Ripshin Lake en route.

Serviceberry bushes bloom atop Little Rock Knob, near Hughes Gap on the Appalachian Trail.

Roan Highlands Area

Appalachian Trail, Grassy Ridge Bald Trail, Overmountain Victory Trail, Yellow Mountain Trail, Hump Mountain Trail and Cloudland Trail

Maps for this area are on pages 192 and 193.

The Highlands of Roan are among the most popular destinations for hikers in the intermountain region. The area including Roan High Knob and adjacent ridges has something for everyone, from the casual windshield tourist to the hardcore Daniel Boone types, including a paved path to accommodate the handicapped at the Rhododendron Gardens. The splendor of rhododendron in bloom in early summer is unsurpassed in the Appalachian Mountains. Open grassy and heath balds on the high crests are some of the best preserved of these rapidly vanishing ecosystems and survey beautiful views year around. Roan High Knob has virgin stands of Canadian type spruce/fir forests, while the lower gaps and slopes offer varied southern hardwoods. Biological

Part of the panorama from near the junction of the Grassy Ridge and Appalachian Trails on the Highlands of Roan.

diversity and dramatic scenery repeatedly draw many hikers back. The Highlands of Roan will occupy a prominent place on any list of the region's most scenic spots.

Someone with limited time to spend in the Appalachian region would have a difficult time finding a better area to explore than that along the **Appalachian Trail** from the Roan High Knob access northward to the U.S. 19-E access.

The **Appalachian Trail** is well traveled, marked with standard white painted blazes, and well maintained in this segment. Walking is fairly easy on the open balds and is moderate through the wooded portions, although there are several strenuous grades.

Appalachian Trail:

Hughes Gap north to Carver's Gap:
Trail segment distance: 4.6 miles, one way.
Difficulty rating: Moderate, strenuous climbs, but a good, clearly-marked path.

Walking north, from the Hughes Gap (Access 1), the Appalachian Trail climbs steadily for nearly 3 miles to the summit of Roan High Knob, at 6,285 feet. All but the strongest hikers will be crawling by the time they reach the summit from this access, there is a climb of more than 2,000 feet.

"Just an opportunity to demonstrate leadership," stated one of my more "gung ho" companions as I lagged far behind on the long climb, panting like a dog. Even the sense of triumph at finally reaching the top was short-lived when another of my "buddies" said:

"Ken, if I had known you were going to get angst like this, I'd have brought you a paper bag to help with your hyperventilation." Two more reasons to start at the top (Access 3), or at Carver's Gap (Access 2) from now on, or to ignore my own advice and hike alone!

En route, the forest changes from Appalachian hardwoods to Canadian type spruce/fir. The numerous dead trees encountered as the altitude increases are attributed to severe weather, acid precipitation, and infestation by Balsam Wooly Aphids.

Similar damage is apparent on all higher peaks in the Appalachians. Annual rainfall on these peaks is greater than eighty inches, which is about double that of the surrounding valleys. Attendant acid deposition, combined with winds that can top 100 miles per hour, extended periods of minus 0 degree temperatures, and imported pests as the Wooly Aphid have left bleaching skeletons of ghost forests here and on Mount Mitchell, Clingman's Dome and other high summits.

The white blazed trail reaches the top of Roan High Knob near Lot #1 in the Rhododendron Gardens area (See Access 3). Detours onto the **Cloudland Trail** and other short walks atop the summit offer additional opportunities to explore beds of Catawba Rhododendron and bogs where iridescent green moss covers the ground like deep pile carpet. Constructed overlooks at the ends of these detours offer expansive vistas of the surrounding mountains; several signs and blazes point them out. A plaque notes the site of the old Cloudland Hotel, which stood on the crest until around 1915.

Continuing northward on the Appalachian Trail from the top of Roan High Knob, the footpath descends back through an evergreen forest to a point near the picnic/parking area at Carver's Gap, a distance of about 1.6 miles. As in approaching the crest from the other side, this is a steep and serpentine course, although here the altitude change is less that 1,000 feet.

Appalachian Trail:

North from Carver's Gap to Yellow Mountain Gap:
Trail segment distance: 4.6 miles, one way.
Difficulty rating: Easy to moderate.

The hike northward on the Appalachian Trail from Carver's Gap (Access 2) begins with a fairly gradual climb up the Round Bald ridge opposite the parking area at the State line. There is a stile at the fence, and white painted blazes are easily picked out on rocks and steps marking the route.

This slope is rimmed by rhododendron bushes, which reach their peak bloom from late June to early July, depending on the spring weather. During this peak, the hillsides are vibrant with their magenta blooms mixed with flame azalea, hawkweed and Gray's Lily. And these are only a few of a wide variety of wildflowers which color the highlands throughout the growing season. The Highlands of Roan are renowned for their unique ecosystems and the profusion of rare plant varieties. Except for the tropical rain forest, this region has the greatest variety of naturally occurring, flowering species on earth.

To help protect the bald from erosion, terrace logs are imbedded into the first hillside, since most foot traffic retreats to automobiles after a short excursion. This slope is typical of the climbs in this segment. Trail distance from Carver's Gap to U.S. Highway 19-E (Access 4) is roughly 13 miles, with no roads crossed in-between. The Yellow Mountain Gap (Access 5) is less used but listed here for those primarily interested in shorter day hikes.

Initially, the trail follows the crest of the balds and offers unlimited vistas of the mountains extending in all directions for as far as the day's humidity will permit. The first hill is Round Bald, then comes Jane Bald, Engine Gap, and the shoulder of Grassy Ridge Bald. The route meanders back and forth across the imaginary line that divides Tennessee and North Carolina.

The Balds are well below the tree line. The exact reason these particular mountain tops are nearly treeless is uncertain, since they have been open throughout written history. Lightning and severe weather have contributed to the gnarled dwarf trees around the summits but are not the sole explanations for the meadows, since many of the bald areas are currently being reclaimed by forest. The highlands may have originally been cleared by fire (either naturally occurring or set by Indian hunters to drive game and improve berry crops) then kept clear by grazing herds of deer, elk, bison and other wildlife.

The fate of the bald areas inside and outside the National Forests is uncertain. Resort and second-home developments are rapidly overwhelming many of the privately-held scenic areas. Inside protected areas, new growth brush and trees that were once limited by browsing animals are becoming overgrown. Controlled burning has been attempted on the Roan Highlands, but whether the advance of forest over the open balds has been arrested is yet to be seen. There is also a debate over whether the balds should be preserved or nature allowed to take its course, now that most of the animals have been removed.

At the top of the third ridge from Carver's Gap, double white blazes and a sign indicate the Appalachian Trail veering to the left along the side of the hill, to the Grassy Ridge Shelter. Another well-used path continues straight along the crest of the bald area, bearing right and more southerly.

This is the **Grassy Ridge Trail**.

The Grassy Ridge Trail: From the Appalachian Trail Junction.

This footpath leads along high crests with beautiful views, through grassy meadows, rhododendron and flame azalea gardens, and in a couple of miles, onto private lands, where rough jeep routes head down opposing slopes to the Roaring Fork and North Carolina Highway 261 areas.

Grassy Ridge has recently been threatened with development, but through the efforts of the Southern Appalachian Highlands Conservancy, Tennessee Senator Jim Sasser, and others concerned with preservation of the balds, at least the summit area is now protected. Grassy Ridge is one of the premier rhododendron viewing areas. Given the views along its 6,000+ foot summit the **Grassy Ridge Trail** is a worthwhile detour from the Appalachian Trail. It also makes an excellent round trip walk in the 5-7 mile range (depending on how far along the ridge you explore) from Carver's Gap.

The **Grassy Ridge Trail** lingers along the higher ground, offering 360 degree panoramas from its buttes. The path is well defined, although not marked, and is rated easy, at least in the summit area. The trail is recommended only from the Appalachian Trail connection and along the crest.

—Continuing north on the Appalachian Trail:

Backpackers on the Grassy Ridge Trail on the Highlands of Roan.

From the rocky pinnacles at the Grassy Ridge/Appalachian Trails junction, the continuing route of the Georgia to Maine footpath can be seen ahead, along Yellow, Little Hump and Hump Mountains. Looking slightly north from due east, it emerges from scrubby woods on the next ridge side and continues up the grassy slopes. The views from these beckoning crests are several miles ahead, and the trail in-between passes mostly through dense forest. The route edges along the shoulder of the ridge to the Grassy Ridge Shelter through dense thickets with small springs and seeps. Through these woods old logging roads are encountered; these roads once descended the Tennessee side of the mountain along Heaton Creek and Sugar Hollow, but they are mostly overgrown now, or fall into the primitive path and game trail categories. In late summer the narrowing Appalachian Trail between the edge of Grassy Ridge Bald and Yellow Mountain Gap can become partly overhung with tall weeds and nettles. This section of the trail is rated moderate, but is mostly downhill until reaching Yellow Mountain Gap.

The Overmountain Victory Trail crosses the white blazed trail at this point and can be followed down the North Carolina slope to Access 5. Alternatively, one can follow the blue trail toward the Appalachian Trail shelter to the Forest Service gravel road, then take the road ½ mile to the parking area.

Overmountain Victory Trail:
From the Appalachian Trail at Yellow Mountain Gap.

Yellow Mountain Gap is the junction of the Appalachian Trail with the **Overmountain Victory Trail**. There are signs indicating the intersecting paths (if they survive the vandals) and pointing to the Yellow Mountain Gap Shelter.

Yellow Mountain Gap was on one of the main branches of ancient Indian War/Trading Paths, connecting the mountain heartland with tribes to the east. Later the trail (known as Bright's Trace) was one of the routes of pioneers settling the Watauga, Holston and Nolichuckey River basins. "Overmountain Victory" refers to the trail used by frontiersmen crossing the gap to join other patriot volunteers at the battle of Kings Mountain during the American Revolution. The gap offers an excellent 180 degree view toward the south.

Blue painted blazes on the southwest side of the gap lead about ¼ mile to a gravel Forest Service Road, then to the Yellow Mountain Gap shelter (an old barn overlooking the next meadow west). But the **Overmountain Victory Trail** (on this side of the gap) does not follow the blue route more than a few feet. At the first turn of the blue route, the ancient path continues straight, toward the valley, along an old fence line and a partly over grown road beside the meadow. This unmarked route is easily followed about ¾ mile, downhill and toward the valley, to the creek and parking area on Roaring Fork Branch (see Access 5 for more details).

On the north side of the gap, an old road swath and rough path descend the ridge to the Hampton Creek area on the Tennessee side of the mountain. Although steep and possibly overgrown during mid-summer, there are occasional blue painted blazes on this route. The path descends onto private lands at the dead end of Hampton Creek Road, 5.5 miles by winding country lane above the town of Roan Mountain.

The Overmountain Victory Trail retraces the historic route of the Revolutionary War patriots from Sycamore Shoals, at Elizabethton, Tennessee, to Kings Mountain on the South Carolina border. Most of the route is over developed roadways, but in this area the travel is still on foot or horseback.

Appalachian Trail:

Continuing north from Yellow Mountain Gap to U.S. 19-E:
Trail segment distance: 8.3 miles, approximate, one way.
Difficulty rating: Moderate.

Map for this segment is on page 193.

Most hikers will be continuing their walk between Carver's Gap and U.S. 19-E at this point, but this access (Access 5) is also an excellent place to begin day hikes to the Yellow and Hump Mountain Balds, or to explore the **Overmountain Victory Loop** around the Yellow Mountain Gap area.

The gap is about ¾ mile from the parking/turnaround, either by the **Overmountain Victory Trail** or the combined closed Forest Service Road and blue blazed Appalachian Trail Shelter spur.

From Yellow Mountain Gap, the Appalachian Trail begins another moderately steep climb of a little over one mile, to near the summit of Yellow Mountain. Initially, the route is adjacent to a large meadow, and alternate paths run parallel. In late summer, this meadow is awash in bright colors of blooming cone flowers, black-eyed susans, asters and other wild flowers. Near the top of this meadow, another branch of the **Overmountain Victory Loop** can be spotted, turning diagonally to the southeast. This branch of the **Victory Loop** travels along the shoulder of the mountain by an old road for about ½ mile; then it winds down through the woods and east side of the meadows to the parking on Roaring Fork Branch (Access 5).

Near the top of the mountain, a rough track turns sharply to the southwest

Summer wildflower meadows near the junction of the Overmountain Victory and Appalachian Trails at Yellow Mountain Gap.

from the Appalachian Trail, going back down the mountain to connect with the **Overmountain Loop**. This provides an alternate route back to the lower meadows or Access 5 on day hikes. Just beyond this point, the route opens up onto Yellow Mountain Bald.

Double white painted blazes mark the Appalachian Trail's turn to follow the ridge shoulder, just below the pinnacle. There is a stile across an old fence here. The jeep road continues past the turn to the summit, only about

100 yards higher on the ridge. This is a rewarding detour from the marked path. At the pinnacle there is an excellent 360 degree panorama, including views of Grandfather Mountain, Table Rock, Hawksbill Mountain, and others to the east. The rocks atop the summit are laced with ferns and blueberry bushes, and look out over the balds toward Hump Mountain to the north.

Also turning from the pinnacle is the **Big Yellow Mountain Trail**. This track turns south from the peak. This route, with over arching brush thickets, is not marked but fairly easy to follow for about a mile, leading to the beautifully preserved balds and dramatic views on Big Yellow Mountain. This area is the heart of the acquisitions of the Southern Appalachians Highlands Conservancy. The **Big Yellow Mountain Trail** can then be followed across the open balds, descending the ridge along the Whitaker Branch Road access from U.S. 19-E. The total distance is estimated at 6 miles, one way.

—Continuing north on the Appalachian Trail from Yellow Mountain:

Returning to the Appalachian Trail, the route is over open meadows for the next 3 miles (approximate), except for a brief stretch of woods approaching Bradley Gap. The wide, easily followed path crosses Little Hump Mountain, descending to Bradley Gap; then makes a fairly strenuous climb of Hump Mountain. Excellent vistas and varied flora are enjoyed all along these open areas. You can view 360 degree sweeps from the cone-shaped Hump Mountain. From this landmark, its distinctive shape visible throughout the region, the course begins its descent to U.S. 19-E near the Tennessee/North Carolina line (Access 4). At 5,587 feet, though, the Hump Mountain summit is an excellent place to take a nice long break.

The views north and south along the Blueridge chain are outstanding. Numerous, unmarked secondary trails branch off from the summit, and at Bradley Gap as well, to little-used access points from each side of the mountain (noted at the end of Access 5). They offer opportunities to explore further around the balds. Some of these connecting paths are:

Old Appalachian Trail Route:

Late in the summer this can be an overgrown, primitive path. It descends from the north side of the Hump Mountain summit to just west of the current Appalachian Trail route at Doll Flats. It also intersects the following unmarked path coming up from the Shell Creek area on the Tennessee side of the mountain.

The view southwest of the Roan Highlands from Little Hump Mountain.

Shell Creek Trail:

This is an old foot path and unmarked Forest Service right-of-way. It crosses private lands and pastures with gates. There is a Forest Service gate restricting traffic, and there is no parking at the end of Shell Creek Road. The narrow paved lane turns from U.S. 19-E at a point 1.8 miles south from the town of Roan Mountain. The route is easily followed by foot travelers, but it is a steep two-mile walk to the Appalachian Trail junction at Doll Flats, or to the abandoned Old Appalachian Trail Route.

There is a similar old trail, still clear enough to walk, that meets the Appalachian Trail near the start of the assent of Hump Mountain on the southwestern slope. It can be spotted leading diagonally through the woods, northward from the meadows. There are no markers, and much of this route is through private pastureland. It meets Shell Creek Road, about ¼ mile below the Forest Service gate for the route above in about 2 miles.

Hump Mountain Trail:

There are also less-traveled routes on the North Carolina side of the mountain. One turns diagonally and eastward from near Bradley Gap. This route, through scrubby Beech woods, skirts along the shoulder of the ridge, thus avoiding the climb up the mountain, and meets the Appalachian Trail again as it descends the summit on the southeastern slope.

From this unmarked junction, fairly clear tracks of an old road can be seen heading down through the open meadow on the southern slope, as the Appalachian Trail loops back northward toward the woods. At the bottom of the meadow, the old road, Forest Service right-of-way continues, flanked by private and public woods, to emerge at the end of Horse Creek Road near U.S. 19-E in about 2 miles.

—Continuing north on the Appalachian Trail from Hump Mountain to U.S. 19-E:

From the meadows around Hump Mountain, the remainder of this Appalachian Trail segment is through mixed hardwoods, except for the fields of Doll Flats where there are good views of the Elk Park area. It is a long steep slope down from Doll Flats to the highway parking area, but it is much better to be coming downhill, since there is an altitude change of more than 2,500 feet in the nearly 4 miles between U.S. 19-E and the summit of Hump Mountain. An Appalachian Trail shelter is located about ½ mile before the highway/parking.

How to Get There

Access 1: Hughes Gap

To meet the Appalachian Trail south of Roan High Knob, the Hughes Gap point is easily reached from the Roan Mountain State Park area. Drive one mile south from the swimming pool area, toward North Carolina, on Tennessee Highway 143. Turn right, onto Cove Road, at the community of Burbank (there are convenience markets and a green street sign at the intersection). Bear right, as the paved road winds uphill, onto Hughes Gap Road. The trail crosses the road at the crest, on the Tennessee/North Carolina line. This point is 3 miles from TN-143, at current end of pavement. The gravel road (returning to pavement in a bit over a mile) can be followed 4.5 miles to NC-226, at Buladean, North Carolina. A right turn onto NC-226 leads 4 miles to another junction with the Appalachian Trail at Iron Mountain Gap, where the road becomes TN-107 traveling toward Unicoi, Tennessee.

There is limited parking along the roadway at Hughes Gap. Trail distances from this point are: To the north: Roan High Knob, 3 miles, and Carver's Gap, 4.6; to the south: Little Rock Knob, 1.3 miles and Clyde Smith Shelter, 2.1; and Iron Mountain Gap, on state routes 107/226, 8.1 miles.

Access 2: Carver's Gap Area

From U.S. Highway 19-E, at the town of Roan Mountain, Tennessee, take TN-143. There is a sign to Roan Mountain State Resort Park, which is passed en route to Carver's Gap.

The State Park offers full camping facilities as well as rental cabins, a restaurant, a swimming pool, a varied summer program of nature walks and campfires, its own system of hiking trails, and a cross-country skiing concession during the winter.

Carver's Gap is 8 miles beyond the park at the crest of the mountain, on the Tennessee/North Carolina line. There is a parking and picnic area at this point. White painted blazes for the **Appalachian Trail** are easily seen ascending the ridge on the east side of the roadway (north on the foot trail). The trail head south is on the paved road that turns to Roan High Knob (there is a sign for Rhododendron Gardens here), just past the parking and picnic area entrance and running westward behind it.

The highway becomes NC-261 at Carver's Gap and is 14 miles from Bakersville, North Carolina.

Grassy Ridge Bald Trail

The Grassy Ridge Bald Trail is a spur turning from the Appalachian Trail atop the third ridge north from Carver's Gap. This summit route can be previewed by looking southeast from the first hilltop (Round Bald) from Carver's Gap, on the Appalachian Trail. Grassy Ridge is the large ridge looming in the south and eastern foregrounds. The trail route is along the open area on the crest profile, and then it descends through rhododendron and brush thickets through the deep gap to the south. There are open pastures at first, then rough wooded tracks which lead down the slope onto private lands in the Roaring Branch Road area and NC-261, near the Glen Ayre community. This trail is only recommended from the Appalachian Trail junction.

The grassy, open balds atop Grassy Ridge are a highly recommended, picturesque walk any time of year, and especially during early summer when rhododendron, blackberry and other flowers are at their peak. The crest makes a fairly easy half day round trip from Carver's Gap. The trail on the ridge is unmarked, but clearly defined, since it receives a lot of foot traffic. The junction with the Appalachian Trail is the point where the white blazes leave the open meadows to descend the ridge shoulder, en route to the Grassy Ridge Shelter. Also, see the Appalachian Trail narrative for this section.

Access 3: Roan High Knob/Rhododendron Gardens Area

Continuing from Carver's Gap, Access 2, turn onto the paved road up the mountain toward Roan High Knob and Rhododendron Gardens. There is a sign at this junction. At 1.7 miles (before reaching the parking lots atop the mountain), there is a turnout on the right side of the road. Parking is limited here, but the white blazes of the **Appalachian Trail** approach the road at this point. Continuing up the road to Lot #1 (the official parking area at the summit), the **Appalachian Trail** also nears the south end of the parking area, close to the rest rooms. From the parking, walk northeastward along a well-traveled path, past the foundations of the old Cloudland Hotel; the white trail markers will be found less than 100 yards from the parking. There are excellent views from this crest.

The **Cloudland Trail** also begins at this parking area and enters the woods on its other end.

Cloudland and Rhododendron Garden Trails

The **Cloudland Trail** travels through the woods parallel to the gravel road that continues from Lot #1, generally to the southwest. Spurs along its course lead out to excellent overlooks. Lush evergreen forest alternates with tree graveyards in sections hit by the Balsam Wooly Aphid. After the gravel roadway ends, the trail continues through the spruce/fir forest to a constructed overlook at the point; the views are excellent. It is rated very easy, and just over one mile total, one way. This area is also popular with cross-country skiers in winter.

The **Rhododendron Gardens Trails** are paved walks through the beds of Catawba Rhododendron. There are two loops in this area less than one mile in combined length, plus a handicapped-accessible segment and self interpretive nature trail, along with picnic tables and rest rooms. Rated very easy.

Access 4: U.S. 19-E

There is a sign for the **Appalachian Trail** and turnout/parking on the south side of U.S. 19-E, at approximately 3.9 miles from the TN-143 junction at the village of Roan Mountain. This access/parking is just before reaching the larger "Welcome to North Carolina" sign, so if you pass it, you went too far.

Access 5: Yellow Mountain Gap, Big Yellow Mountain and Hump Mountain points

Since the **Appalachian Trail** doesn't cross any roads in the 12.9 miles between Carver's Gap and U.S. 19-E, this section notes less used, secondary footpaths from both the Tennessee and North Carolina sides of the Roan Highlands. The best, and easiest to locate, of these connectors is from Yellow Mountain Gap on the North Carolina side.

As noted in the Appalachian Trail narrative, Yellow Mountain Gap can be approached from either Tennessee or North Carolina, but the best trail, largest parking, and clearest landmarks are found on the North Carolina approach up Roaring Fork Creek Road. It is a favorite starting point for day walks on the highlands.

Traveling south from the Cranberry Community, at the junction of U.S. 19-E/NC-194, Roaring Fork Creek intersects the highway in approximately

8.5 miles. There is a historical marker noting the Yellow Mountain Road at this point.

There are two other rural roads intersecting U.S. 19-E that are worth noting en route, since they are also used to reach upper parts of the mountains: 1) Secondary Road NC-1199 (3.5 miles from Cranberry Junction) dead ends at the foot of Hump Mountain. A rough Forest Service right-of-way continues behind a barn at the end of the public road and has been used by hikers to climb Hump Mountain via Horse Creek. 2) Secondary Road NC-1136, Whitaker Branch Road (6.5 miles from 19-E/194), dead ends at the base of Big Yellow Mountain. There are signs noting the properties of the Southern Appalachian Highlands Conservancy at the end of the public road, and old tracks can be walked up to the open balds atop the mountain and to the Yellow Mountain Trail. More on these later.

Back to the Yellow Mountain Gap access:

Turn from U.S. 19-E onto Roaring Fork Road. Bear right, keeping to the paved road, traveling up the hollow and along the main stream. Currently, the pavement ends in 3.6 miles, and the parking/gates/turn around are reached at 5 miles from U.S. 19-E. There are two white gates at this point, one on the right of the roadway beside the creek, and the other bars the road continuing straight (this gate is usually closed to vehicles, but may be left open during hunting season). This turnaround has plentiful parking space and is the starting point of listed walks for Yellow Mountain Gap, as follows:

Alternative 1:

The gravel Forest Service Road, which continues straight beyond the turnaround, ends in about ½ mile at the blue marked Appalachian Trail spur. Turning left into the meadow leads to the Yellow Mountain Gap Shelter. Turning right onto the blue trail leads ¼ mile uphill to the gap and junctions with the **Appalachian Trail,** the **Overmountain Victory Trail,** and the **Overmountain Victory Loop** around the meadows.

Alternative 2:

The white gate on the east side of the turnaround/parking is the trail head for the **Overmountain Victory Loop**, one of the Pisgah National Forest system of hiker trails. A closed jeep road follows the creek through meadows and woods, directly behind the gate. This wide, unmarked route is fairly clear and easy to follow, but has moderate climbing along the shoulder of

Yellow Mountain. The Overmountain Victory Loop circles the meadows along their northern and eastern sides, although mostly through the forest. About midway up the mountain (an estimated ¾ mile from the parking), there is a sharp fork in the trail. The right branch is a strenuous ½ mile climb to the pinnacle of Little Yellow Mountain and the junction with the **Appalachian Trail** (noted in Appalachian Trail narrative). The route continuing straight from the fork toward the open meadows intersects the **Appalachian Trail** in about ¼ mile, near the top of the fields. The white marked route can be followed downhill to Yellow Mountain Gap; then either the blue marked trail to the closed Forest Service Road, or an old track along the fence and edge of the meadow, will complete the loop back to the parking.

Alternative 3:

A more direct route to the gap from the parking follows the **Overmountain Victory Trail**. About midway between the two gates, a narrow path turns diagonally toward Yellow Mountain Gap. Traveling generally northward, it is also unmarked, and can be partly obscured by low brush and weeds in midsummer near the parking/turnaround. Beginning with tank trap type barriers as a narrow footpath, it picks up an old cut road along the edge of the fields in about 200 yards. The old road is then easy to follow to the gap. The grade is gradual for its estimated ¾ mile climb to the gap and the intersections with the blue and white marked paths there.

Big Yellow Mountain Trail: Via Whitaker Branch

Approximately 6.5 miles south from Cranberry, North Carolina, and the NC-194/US-19-E junction, Whitaker Branch Road turns from U.S. 19-E. A small sign between the Pleasant Hill Church and the volunteer fire department notes it as Route 1136. The road may become difficult to travel in bad weather in about a mile, as it begins to climb this shoulder of Big Yellow Mountain. There is a small cemetery and roadside parking where the road heads uphill. Beginning the walk here (although it may be possible to drive to the edge of the Southern Highlands Conservancy property), the rough public road leads along the edge of farm pastures and private property for another ½ mile or so.

There are small signs noting the edge of the Conservancy preserve. A clear track continues uphill, through the woods, for an estimated 2 miles, until the open balds of Big Yellow Mountain are reached. The climb is fairly steady,

The Appalachian Bald of Big Yellow Mountain on the Yellow Mountain Trail.

but gradual, and the trail easily followed, although not marked. The meadows atop the mountain present some of the best views in the region.

Along the meadows atop the mountain, a clear trail continues northward along the crest. A gate separates the open bald of Big Yellow Mountain and the ridge (which is covered with scrubby new growth) connecting it with the pinnacle of Little Yellow Mountain. This gate provides a dramatic illustration of the benefits of even limited livestock grazing in preserving the balds. The area on one side of the barrier has been used as summer pasture in recent years, while the other has become a tangled thicket. From the gate the trail continues through an overarching tangle for another mile, along the saddle of ridges, to the Little Yellow Mountain pinnacle and a junction with the white blazed **Appalachian Trail** (this junction is also noted in Appalachian Trail narrative). Total distance, roughly estimated, from the cemetery turn-out to intersecting the white marked path, is 6 miles.

Hump Mountain Trail: Via Horse Creek

Travel 3.5 miles south from the Cranberry, North Carolina, 194/19-E junction. Turn right onto NC-1199, then onto gravel NC-1167 in 0.3 mile. The trail turns right from the roadway in 0.6 mile, just before it dead ends.

There is a "No Parking" sign here. This is a narrow dirt lane through private lands, but there is limited roadside parking back down the hill.

The trail up this side of the ridge begins by fording the creek and following the old Forest Service right-of-way through mixed private and public holdings. A small cemetery and several smaller waterfalls and cascades are passed along the old cut road as it climbs, with switchbacks, up the forested ridge. There are no markers, but the track is clear and well traveled. After an estimated 1.5 miles of steady climbing, the scraggly brush of the edge of the balds are encountered, as are forks in the tracks. One branch turns westward along the shoulder of Hump Mountain to Bradley Gap and intersects the **Appalachian Trail** just before its assent of the pinnacle of Hump Mountain. The fork continuing up the open area of balds (and toward the eastern side of the summit) also intersects the Appalachian Trail as it descends the peak. Other branches in the trails extend over the balds eastward.

A tired hiker takes a break atop Hump Mountain.

Appalachian Trail

Big Pine/Walnut Mountain Areas:
U.S. 19-E to Walnut Mountain Road
Trail segment distance: 6.7 miles one way.
Difficulty rating: Moderate.

Map for this area is on page 193.

The Big Pine Mountain segment of the Appalachian Trail (from U.S. 19-E to Walnut Mountain Road) is used little except by through hikers on the Maine to Georgia footpath. This sector begins by climbing Buck Mountain from U.S. 19-E, then passes through old fields and mixed regrowth woods. The first half of this segment is through mixed private and public holdings. Beginning the walk on the north side of U.S. 19-E (See Access 3 or 4 in the Roan Highlands chapter), the path follows Bear Branch Road 0.2 mile then turns left onto an old road.

There is considerable climbing on this south-facing slope, but near the summit there are spectacular panoramas from old meadows. Standing to the east is the distinctive profile of Grandfather Mountain appearing as a reposing old man. The cone-shaped profile of Hump Mountain, with its grassy bald, looms on the southern horizon; and looking westward along the horizon, Yellow Mountain and other landmarks of the Roan Highlands (passed in the previous section of the Appalachian Trail) are visible.

At the top of the mountain (about 2.5 miles from U.S. 19-E), the trail emerges onto a gravel lane near Isaacs Cemetery (See Access 2). The route continues along this lane for approximately 100 yards then turns left onto the paved Buck Mountain Road. The white blazed path returns to the woods for about ¼ mile, then it emerges onto another paved country lane, Campbell Hollow Road. This road is followed for about ½ mile and then turns into the quiet, mature woodlands of the National Forest for a loop through the Sugar Hollow area. The path travels up and down low ridges and along old road beds and has several stream crossings as the route meanders to the foot of Big Pine Mountain. A spur to the Appalachian Trail shelter is passed at about 1 mile from Campbell Hollow Road. The trail turns westward along a moderately graded slope up Big Pine Mountain.

The stroll along the summit is beneath tall pines and hardwoods. Descending the slope on the southwest side of the mountain, a relic of Appalachian lore may be spotted in the rhododendron thickets to the left of the trail: an abandoned moonshine still. Apparently revenuers ended its usefulness, since there are large gashes in its drums, but it was a crude affair compared to the finely-crafted, copper variety that once flourished in the dark hollows. However, it appears to be the genuine article, just the sort of discovery to get a nosy hiker shot a generation or two ago. Pieces of small gauge rails had been used to support the cooker over the fire, and a nearby wet weather spring was used to condense the liquid corn. The rails are remnants of the small lines and logging spurs which once operated throughout the mountains of northeastern Tennessee and western North Carolina, the most famous of which was the "Tweetsie."

The making of whiskey, brandy and apple jack was once an art in this region. Many Scottish and Irish immigrants maintained a long tradition of distilling the finest spirits. Some old-timers still bitterly denounce the politics that killed one of the region's major cottage industries (or at least lowered the quality of its product in recent years, a development caused by the furtive nature of the business). Some claim that there was a conspiracy by the coal and timber barons to keep the mountaineer poor and subservient, since the only profitable way to take produce to markets that were far away was in refined form.

"Rotgut" is still made, marijuana patches are tended, poaching and other illegal activities still go on in isolated coves like this. It is unlikely that hikers on established trails will ever encounter contraband in the forest, but the best advice is not to get too suspicious and mind your own business.

Much of the Appalachian Trail in this area has recently been rerouted to keep more to the public forest. However, there are notices in the area shelters warning of thefts and vandalism in this segment of the trail.

A nearby point of interest is the 85-foot high Elk River Falls. In the Sugar Hollow area, there is a maze of old game and timbering tracks (all unmarked) which meander in the direction of the river. Maps of the area show an old road leading to the falls area in about 1 mile, but some exploring would be required to tell which one. Directions by road to the falls are listed below.

The loop through Sugar Hollow and over Big Pine Mountain is a well maintained, clearly defined, single-file path which emerges onto gravel Walnut Mountain Road, Access 1.

How to Get There

Maps for this segment are on pages 192 and 193.

Access 1 is also the start of the White Rocks Mountain segment of the Appalachian Trail and can be used as an access to the upper part of the Laurel Fork Trail. To approach this point from the other direction, refer to the Laurel Fork/Dennis Cove chapter.

Access 1: Walnut Mountain Road

From the Roan Mountain U.S. 19-E/TN-143 junction, drive 1.5 miles east and turn left onto paved Buck Mountain Road (beside the Roan Mountain Animal Hospital). Proceed up the mountain; bear right at the first two paved roads; pass the High Point Church (on the right); and turn left onto the paved road at 3.5 miles from U.S. 19-E. There is a sign for Kinsey Garden Center at this junction. The Laurel Fork Church is passed shortly after the turn and the Appalachian Trail crosses the lane (which currently turns to gravel en route) at 1.5 miles. This crossing is hard to spot, since there is no parking area or other signs. However, if you watch closely, the white blazes are visible on trees heading into the woods on either side of the narrow roadway. There is room for a vehicle or two at nearby turnouts.

Access 2: Buck Mountain Area

Follow directions for Access 1 to a point 3.5 miles from U.S. 19-E, but instead of turning northward past the Laurel Fork Church, continue straight for another ½ mile. White blazes join the road near a small white frame Baptist Church on the left. The trail then turns onto the single track gravel lane leading to the Isaacs Cemetery (a right turn from the pavement).

Access 3: U.S. Highway 19-E

The Appalachian Trail crosses the major highway in this area (U.S. 19-E) at approximately 3.9 miles east from the town of Roan Mountain. There is a sign and large turnout/parking for the trail. If you cross the North Carolina, line you missed it. The trail north begins a short distance up the intersecting Bear Branch Road (where the white blazes are visible).

Elk River Falls Directions:

Traveling east from the state lines on U.S. 19-E, Old Highway 194 (marked by a sign) turns left onto a narrow lane turn near Elk Park, North Carolina. Turn left again in less than ¼ mile, onto Elk River Road and follow it for 4 miles to its end at a parking/picnic area at Elk River Falls. There are signs at the turns for the commercial Elk River Campground.

From the parking area there is a short path to the falls. A rough forest road and developed hiker paths continue along the river for about a mile, but terminate at a ford and thickets blocking access into the gorge.

View of Hump Mountain and the Roan Highlands from Buck Mountain.

Elk River Falls, a short drive from U.S. 19-E near the Tennessee/North Carolina line.

Appalachian Trail

White Rocks Mountain:
North from Walnut Mountain Road to Dennis Cove
    Trail segment distance: 12.3 miles, one way.
    Difficulty rating: Moderate.
    Connecting trails: Laurel Fork, Lacy Trap Ridge and Leonard Branch.

Circuit hikes which link the Appalachian and Laurel Fork Trails are possible in this area. They can be of varied length. Other attractions include views from old fields, views from the fire tower atop White Rocks Mountain, and and a view of Coon Den Falls near the segment end.

The first 5 miles or so are through areas of boggy streams with several crossings. Then the route climbs the main slope of White Rocks Mountain and follows the ridge line. Most of the inclines coming from this end are gradual, but near Dennis Cove the hill is steep, with several switchbacks.

How to Get There

Maps for this area are on pages 192 and 193.

Access by road for this segment of the Appalachian Trail is available on both sides of the Mountain. The south side of the crest is reached by Access 3 (described below). Points on the north side are the same as those listed for the Big Pine Mountain segment and the Laurel Fork Trail. Briefly the main road approaches are:

Access 1: Walnut Mountain Road

Turn left onto Buck Mountain Road, 1.5 miles east of Roan Mountain on U.S. 19-E (which is beside Roan Mt. Animal Hospital); bear right up the mountain; turn left onto Walnut Mountain Road at 3.5 miles, and go past Laurel Fork Church. The Appalachian Trail crosses the lane (which turns to gravel en route) at 1.5 miles.

Access 2: Dennis Cove Road

From the US-321/19-E junction at Hampton, drive north on US-321 for 0.8 mile, then turn right beside Citizens Bank onto Dennis Cove Road; and the Appalachian Trail is crossed in 4.8 miles. For other points see Frog Level and Cherry Flats entries for Laurel Fork Trail.

Access 3: From Roan Mountain Area/south slope of White Rocks Mountain.

Railroad Grade Road turns north from U.S. 19-E at 10.8 miles from the US-321/19-E junction at Hampton, or 2.0 miles from the U.S. 19-E/TN-143 junction at Roan Mountain. There is a sign for the Tennessee Department of Corrections Work Camp (Carter County). Drive 2.2 miles (passing the prison entrance on the way) and turn right onto a single track road. The pavement ends in 0.5 mile, where an orange Forest Service gate is encountered. If the gate is open, a four wheel drive or all-terrain Vehicle might make it to the top of the mountain, although it would be rough going. From the gate it is a steep 2 mile walk (estimated) to the summit and junction with the Appalachian Trail.

This section of the Appalachian Trail is part of the area maintained by the Tennessee Eastman Hiking Club. It is well cared for and well marked. The course is laid out to control erosion more than for hiker comfort; consideration was also given to keeping the route on the public domain, as much as possible. There are no particular difficulties along this link, although the climb up from Dennis Cove on the reverse course is strenuous, gaining over 1,000 feet in about 1.6 miles.

Beginning at Walnut Mountain Road, the single file path is through marshy areas and low ridges. Stream crossings include the head branches of the Laurel Fork Creek with small cascades. There are several side paths and old roads, with a new graveled logging road crossed in about 3 miles. This timber access road is heavily used due to large areas of clear cutting along the Laurel Fork watershed. A turn south on it leads about ½ mile to Buck Mountain Road. Northward along the road the **Laurel Fork Trail** can be found down the ridge by side paths.

From the logging access road, the marked trail leads over more low ridges and boggy areas for about 3 miles of relatively short and easy inclines. A fairly steep climb then leads up the main slopes of White Rocks Mountain and along its crest for about 4 miles. The Moreland Gap Shelter is in the first high gap, about 7 miles from Walnut Mountain Road. Most of the views are screened or totally blocked by trees, until an open field near the fire tower is reached. At this gap the **Leonards Branch Trail** turns into the field, descending to the above mentioned logging road and onto Laurel Fork Creek. Also in this saddle, the road from the south side of the mountain (Access 3) enters. The **Lacy Trap Trail** intersects the marked trail in about ¼ mile en route to the fire tower. There are excellent views from the tower steps, but the deck and cabin are closed.

Nearing the bottom of the mountain on the Dennis Cove end, a blue blazed path leads to Coon Den Falls. Slender cascades in the 50 foot range are a short detour.

Early European chroniclers of the Indians of this region often romanticized them as princes of the forest who were sensitive to the spiritual and natural world which were overlooked by the white man in his rush to conquer a vast continent. This romantic view was partly true. Without a written language, narrative skills were cultivated to a fine art, just as many old-timers today have vivid imagery and storytelling skills that are being rediscovered. Elders of the Cherokee and other woodland nations passed much of their knowledge to succeeding generations through myths and legends. Much of this lore revolves around quiet places like the pools and streams of the deep forest, where an aura might exist or a passage between the present world and the spirit world might be present. Many of the stories reflect an idea of oneness with "The Grandmother Earth," that every plant and animal has a special place in nature, and that even rocks have spirits to be respected.

Their languages provide names for many streams in our region, often lending lyric qualities that characterize the personalities of rivers which carry them. Sounds in the name Watauga (from the nearby river and lake), for example, evoke an image of a shining, whispering stream, while other names with harder sounds (such as Chatooga or Nolichuckey) bring to mind a rushing torrent. I doubt that the Amerind name for these falls would have carried the hard consonants of "Coon Den Branch." Theirs would probably make the babble of this brook seem smoother.

Appalachian Trail

Watauga Lake and Laurel Fork:
North from Dennis Cove to Iron Mountain.
Including Laurel Fork Falls, Pond Mountain Wilderness Area, and Watauga Lake.

Trail segment distance: 14.3 miles, one way.
Difficulty rating: Moderate in Laurel Fork gorge, difficult climb on Pond Mountain, and easy around Watauga lake.
Connecting Routes: Laurel Fork Trail and primitive Pond Mountain and Bear Stand Trails.

The Appalachian Trail in this segment passes through the dramatic scenery of Laurel Fork gorge with its large waterfall. This narrow canyon has steep slopes and sheer cliffs of 150 feet or more in places. There is a great variety of flowering shrubs and trees in early summer, including pink, purple and white rhododendron, dogwood, service berry, mountain laurel, and flame azalea. The narrow defile is entered on the Dennis Cove end, traveling downstream through an old logging railroad cut, which is followed for about the first mile. The recently designated Pond Mountain Wilderness Area (which restricts further road and development inside its 4,365 acres) is entered in about ½ mile. At about one mile the trail turns sharply downhill into the gorge. A secondary trail continues straight and may be used during flood stage.

The trail arrives at the falls basin after a steep descent. The falls are about 1.3 miles from Dennis Cove Road (see the Laurel Fork chapter for the approach upstream). Laurel Fork Falls are a popular weekend excursion, and they are beautiful. The large pool at their bottom is used as a swimming hole by those who can stand the cold water in summer, although swimming is not recommended, since there is a slippery, rocky bottom in addition to chilly temperatures. The falls are in two stages and drop a total of around 75 feet.

From the falls the white blazed trail continues downstream, curling around boulders and a cliff shelf to return to the old rail bed. At about ½ mile below the falls, the white blazes lead up the steep gorge wall, away from the old road bed to the trail shelter atop the ridge. Blue blazes and a sign mark the

Laurel Fork Falls which can be reached from either the Dennis Cove area or U.S. 321 along the Appalachian and Laurel Fork Trails.

detour to the shelter. The path then runs along the sharp, rocky spine of the hill, which offers excellent views of the gorge, then returns to the ravine for another 0.7 mile, crossing excellent bridges over the stream before turning back uphill for a tour of the ridges below Pond Mountain. The blue blazed trail continuing along the old road bed is the **Laurel Fork Trail**, and it leads about one mile to US-321.

Continuing northward on the Appalachian Trail, there is serious climbing and steep descents ahead as the trail has a net gain in altitude of more than 1,500 feet from both the lake and gorge ends. The remaining 7 miles to U.S. 321 is densely wooded and, although there are tantalizing glimpses of the lake and surrounding mountains, there are few unobstructed views. Atop the ridges there are 3 to 4 miles of relatively easy walking before more steep grades are encountered. About 3.5 miles from Laurel Fork, there are rough trails intersecting above the Pond Flats area and the trail shelter. These primitive routes lead to near the summit and the **Pond Mountain Trail** via the **Bear Stand Trail**, which turns diagonally along the ridge toward USFS-50. These routes may be overgrown in summer. The Appalachian Trail currently reaches US-321 from across the Rat Branch boat ramp.

Note planned trail rerouting: The Appalachian Trail is to again be rerouted in this area. The new route will cross US-321 at the Shook Branch Recreation Area beside Watauga Lake (about one mile nearer Hampton) and will cut 3 miles from the current distance. The new route may be open by late 1992.

From the current Rat Branch road crossing, the continuing white blazed trail edges along the woods and recreation areas between the highway and the lake. At Shook Branch, the white trail markers are near the entrance gate and grassy picnic area of the park and run parallel to the beach. The southwest tip of the impoundment is skirted, and a small road and fishing trails are crossed near the heavily used lake side. The trail also crosses near the front yards of a couple of houses before getting into the TVA pines and then returning to mixed native hardwoods. There are dense understory growths of holly through this section. The white marked path is totally within the forest for the 2 mile stroll between the lakeside recreation area and the dam. The trail shelter is about midway in this link.

There are unmarked side paths leading to little-used lake coves with beautiful views at several points. These are mostly rough fishing spurs and can also be followed along the lakeshore where the banks are not too steep. The slopes down to the lake are abrupt at many of these points, and the water rapidly reaches depths of 150 feet or more in the man-made reservoir.

Appalachian Trail hikers are allowed to cross the dam, normally closed to the public, to reach Watauga Dam Road and the foot of Iron Mountain.

How to Get There

Maps for this segment are on pages 192 and 194.

Access 1: Dennis Cove Road

From the US-321/19-E junction at Hampton, drive east toward Boone and Mountain City on US-321; turn right at 0.8 miles, beside Citizens Bank; then drive 4.8 miles on a narrow paved road to the parking area.

Access 2: U.S. 321 at Rat Branch

From the US-321/19-E junction, drive east on US-321, pass the turn to Dennis Cove at 0.8 miles; note the parking on right, at 1.2 miles (this is the blue blazed trail head up Laurel Fork gorge); note the Shook Branch Recreation Area and lake on the left at 3.5 miles (this will be the crossing

A fisherman in the early morning fog of Watauga Lake at the Rat Branch Access of the Appalachian Trail.

of the planned trail rerouting in area when completed, the white blazes being near the entrance. The Rat Branch boat launch site is at 3.9 miles. The trail south is behind the guard rail on the south side of the highway; the trail north is between the lake and highway.

Access 3: Watauga Dam Road

There are TVA signs on US-321/19-E near Elizabethton and Valley Forge for Watauga Dam. On the Elizabethton bypass Siam Road leads to the river and then goes upstream to the dam. Picturesque Little Wilbur Lake is passed en route, and the white trail blazes are visible at the top of the ridge before reaching the dam's visitor center and parking lot.

A winter view of Watauga Lake, a short detour from the Appalachian Trail.

Laurel Fork/Dennis Cove Areas

Including the Laurel Fork Trail, Lacy Trap/Leonard Branch Trails and Appalachian Trail Connections

Map for this segment is on page 192.

The Laurel Fork and Dennis Cove areas offer several hiker trails, with ratings from relatively easy to moderately difficult. The paths span a variety of woodlands, ranging from high, ridge line vistas to tumbling creeks and waterfalls, including the beautiful Laurel Fork Falls.

Trails is this section may be linked with the Appalachian Trail in the preceding White Rocks Mountain to Watauga Lake segments, for excellent circuit or day trips.

Laurel Fork Trail
Trail distance: 12 miles, one way.
Difficulty rating: Mostly moderate.

This route follows Laurel Fork Creek in the Cherokee National Forest. Its more popular sections are wide, well-traveled, casual strolls, especially to Laurel Fork Falls and smaller falls near Dennis Cove. The route becomes more challenging, with several stream crossings on its upper sections, but each segment has appeal to different groups.

Its total distance is in the 12 mile range, depending on which upper access point is used. There are three main segments:

1) Lower Laurel Fork Trail

The lower section includes the main Laurel Fork Falls and is one of the most popular walks in the region. Rated easy to moderate, it parallels the creek via an old railroad bed for most of its 3.5 miles. This part of the foot trail is well marked, first with blue painted blazes near the US-321 start, and then with white painted markers after its junction with the Appalachian Trail at approximately one mile from the lower trail head.

The serpentine course of the Appalachian Trail between Watauga Lake and Laurel Fork Falls, near the junction with the Laurel Fork Trail.

Bridges have been erected at the two stream crossings. Most of the inclines are gradual. The **Appalachian Trail** is encountered in less than one mile. Trail markings change from blue to white at this point. A left turn onto the white route here would lead north to the Rat Branch Access, in around 6 miles of moderate to strenuous trail (See Access 1 and Appalachian Trail section for more details). Continue along the stream for about ¼ mile following the white blazes, until double white blazes indicate a sharp turn in the main route.

The Appalachian Trail turns steeply uphill at this point, crossing a narrow ridge and reaching the Laurel Fork shelter. This is a fairly steep climb, but there are good views from the rocky ridge spine. The Laurel Fork trail continues straight as an unmarked path but is easily followed on upstream. The trails rejoin in about ½ mile, as the white route descends the southern

Laurel Fork Falls, a little over one mile from Dennis Cove Road.

shoulder of the ridge. Please note, however, that this secondary route may be dangerous and impassable during periods of high water, since it is just above stream level.

Several years ago the Appalachian Trail also followed this lower route along the rocky stream bank. This is a slightly shorter route to the falls, July 15, 1992 and easier when dry. After rejoining the white route, the remaining ½ mile to the falls requires some scrambling over roots and rocks. The falls are about 2.4 miles from the highway by the Laurel Fork Trail.

From the base of the Laurel Fork Falls it is possible, although not recommended, for braver souls to climb around the falls by primitive paths, and on up the creek. Most folks will opt for the main white-marked trail as it climbs out of the gorge by the steep switchback up the ridge, and then goes on to Dennis Cove Road (Access 2) in slightly over one mile.

2) Laurel Fork Trail: Dennis Cove to Frog Level

Continuing from the Dennis Cove Road junction with the Appalachian Trail: Left, along the narrow paved road, leads to the Dennis Cove Campground/

Upstream from the Dennis Cove Recreation Area on the Laurel Fork Trail, a fisherman tries his luck.

Picnic Area in one mile. Blue blazes are visible on fence posts along the roadway for the first 0.7 mile; this secondary route is the old Appalachian Trail. It turns right from the lane, into the woods, for Coon Den Falls and another junction with the Appalachian Trail on this slope of White Rocks Mountain. Just before reaching the bridge at the campground, Access 3 (with an orange Forest Service Gate) is on the right side of the road, near the creek (See Access 3).

This segment of Laurel Fork Trail starts behind the gate. Estimated at 3 miles, this section contains some difficult and uncertain trails, especially during high water seasons. En route to Frog Level (Access 4), the path passes two beautiful smaller falls and numerous pools and cascades. Route markings are sporadic, and foot logs and stepping stones are intermittent. The two smaller falls are popular summer walks for families and fishermen; the path can be rated moderate to these points (for about the first mile). From the falls to Frog Level, some skirting above the falls and obstacles, as well as some wading and playing Daniel Boone, may be anticipated.

The landmarks at Frog Level are the wide, planted meadows for wildlife. If you look around a bit, hiker-only trail signs can be found for the **Leonard Branch** and **Lacy Trap Trails**. These more difficult rated trails depart from the meadows for climbs up White Rocks Mountain and junctions with the Appalachian Trail on the crest.

The turn to the Frog Level Access is very difficult to spot. It is on the left bank of the main stream where an old jeep road comes into the meadows and a smaller stream intersects. The parking/turnaround is 200-300 yards along this road and stream.

These segments are not recommended during periods of heavy rains.

3) Upper Laurel Fork Trail: Frog Level to Cherry Flats

Continuing on the Laurel Fork Trail: The distance from the Frog Level Access (Access 5) to the Cherry Flats Access (Access 6) is estimated at 5 miles. The walking is very easy along an old railroad bed, but there are several stream crossings which increase the difficulty. There are no bridges, foot logs have washed away, and stepping stones are inadequate to prevent wet feet. When the water is low, however, this is one of the most pleasant walks in the region. There are numerous smaller waterfalls, cascades, quiet pools and sliding rocks. It is little used except for an occasional fisherman. This is a designated trout stream and fishing regulations and limits are posted.

There are occasional yellow painted diamond blazes along the route, but it is a wide, easily followed route where they are absent. After about 4½ miles of splashing back and forth through the creek (generally traveling south

A small waterfall on the upper Laurel Fork Trail near the Cherry Flats area.

and southeast), the route becomes a closed jeep road and turns more east/ northeast along a low ridge. This leads away from the main creek, along a small branch and bogs to a gate and parking/turnaround for USFS-50-A, in about ½ mile.

Connecting route to the Appalachian Trail

Since the route of the Laurel Fork Trail is usually within a few yards of the creek, it is fairly easy to spot the last crossing when coming upstream. About 100 yards downtrail and stream from the ford, a couple of paths can be seen turning west. These lead to a wide gravel logging road no more than one hundred yards above Laurel Fork.

A left turn onto the new gravel road leads to a junction of the Appalachian Trail in less than one mile. White trail blazes can be seen at the crossing. From here the Appalachian Trail begins its ascent of White Rocks Mountain, traveling north; or, traveling south on the footpath to Access 7. The opposite direction on the gravel surface leads for several miles along the shoulder of White Rocks Mountain, generally toward the northwest. The logging road runs roughly parallel to both the Appalachian and Laurel Fork routes.

The **Leonard Branch Trail** is fairly easily spotted as it turns toward the mountain summit after about 5 miles (roughly) of following the winding lane.

Leonard Branch Trail is wide and clear, although steep, from the road to the summit, since it is used by ATV's and off-road bikers. The Appalachian Trail crosses at the Summit.

Leonard Branch and Lacy Trap Trails

These secondary trails once made several circuit and day hikes possible by connecting the **Laurel Fork Trail** and **Appalachian Trail** from the Frog Level area to the crest of White Rocks Mountain. The foot paths are still there and, with some exploring, can still be linked with the more popular routes. The routes are little used, however, and may be overgrown in summer. Always hard to find at the Frog Level end, they have now been dissected by a logging road midway up the mountain. Both routes are estimated at 2 miles and are fairly difficult and steep.

Both routes are fairly easy to spot atop the mountain when walking the **Appalachian Trail**. They are generally clear in cooler months, since they receive foot traffic by hunters.

The **Lacy Trap Trail** is a wide, abandoned road turning sharply downhill and generally northeastward from the white marked route, about 300 yards south of the old fire tower on the crest. There are no signs or blazes, but there are tank-trap type barriers to stop vehicle traffic. From the bottom this trail can be located in the wide fields along Laurel Fork gorge by looking for the hiker trail sign in the larger meadow, or by locating the man-made pond in the larger field. The trail fork leads into the woods directly behind the pond. An old apple tree at this junction has delicious fruit on it in the fall (at least above the height that the deer can reach).

The **Leonard Branch Trail** can be found atop the mountain, about ¼ mile farther south on the white marked route. Look for it in the clearing at the gap where an old road crosses the crest (this old jeep road is listed in the Appalachian Trail Access points for this area). The old graded road turns diagonally from the main trail to the southeast. The route is clear and easy to follow to the logging road (mentioned earlier) about one mile down the mountain since it is a horse designated route and has illegal ATV use. From the Frog Level end, things are more difficult. There is a sign for Leonard Branch on Laurel Fork Creek, and blazes lead a short way into the woods before becoming a primitive maze of paths through the laurel thickets. Good luck.

How to Get There

Map for this area is on page 192.

Laurel Fork/Dennis Cove Area: From Elizabethton, Tennessee

Follow the combined U.S. 19-E/321 southeast, toward Boone and Roan Mountain. At Hampton the routes separate. Turn left, following US-321/67. Note your mileage at this point, to aid in selecting the parking/access point you plan to use. (Access to upper parts of the trail leave U.S. 19-E near the town of Roan Mountain—See Access 6 directions.)

Access 1: Lower Laurel Fork Creek

From the division of U.S. 19-E/321, travel 1.1 miles east on US-321. Dennis Cove Road, to Access 2, is passed en route. Parking for the lower part of the **Laurel Fork Trail** is on the right, just across a small concrete bridge. This is a popular walk, and the parking is easily spotted. The trail head is just beyond the wooden barriers, and blue painted blazes for the path are visible. This is the route once followed by the Appalachian Trail. The rerouted Maine to Georgia footpath is intersected in about one mile.

Access 2: Laurel Fork Falls from Dennis Cove Road

Dennis Cove Road turns right from US-321, 0.8 mile from the 19-E division, beside the Citizens Bank.

This steep, narrow, winding mountain road, with barely enough room for two cars to pass (not suited for recreational vehicles and trailers, although some insist on using it for such) is paved and leads 4.1 miles to the parking area for the Appalachian Trail and Laurel Fork Falls. This parking area, which is on the left side of the roadway, will accommodate several cars, and the white blazes of the trail can be noted.

Going north on the **Appalachian Trail**, you will reach Laurel Fork Falls in slightly over one mile.

South on the **Appalachian Trail** (directly across the road from this parking/access) leads through the woods, with hard climbs and switchbacks, up White Rocks Mountain to an old fire tower on its crest.

Alternate trail: Blue painted blazes will also be noted at this point and along the roadway. This is the old route of the Appalachian Trail, and it turns into the woods in 0.7 mile, but there is no parking provided at this departure. This path rejoins the Appalachian Trail on the hillside, and the Laurel Fork route continues along the roadway.

Access 3: Laurel Fork Trail from Dennis Cove Recreation Area

Continuing along Dennis Cove Road from Access 2, the Dennis Cove Picnic Area and Campground is nearly one mile from the Laurel Fork Falls parking (5 miles total from U.S. 321). Parking for this access is in the picnic area. There are short paths upstream on the same side of the creek as the picnic/ camping area, but the main Laurel Fork Trail is on the other side of the stream. For the trail head, walk back across the bridge to the orange Forest Service gate.

Access 4: Laurel Fork Trail from Frog Level

Continuing on Dennis Cove Road from the picnic/camping area (Access 3): Travel 2 miles to the top of the ridge. En route the road becomes the well-maintained gravel USFS Route 50. At the crest a single track road, USFS 50-F (the sign had been destroyed at my latest visit), turns right from the main track and descends to a parking/turnaround reached in 2.2 miles. Also at the crest closed USFS-50-E can be noted turning left from the main track. There is a hiker-only trail notice behind the earth-mound barriers. This is the trail head for the **Pond Mountain** and **Bear Stand Trails** (see Watauga Lake area).

From the Frog Level parking, a shallow brook and trail leads one quarter mile to the main Laurel Fork Creek. There are signs noting the trail heads and partial trail markings (yellow painted and metal diamond blazes). Unfortunately, these are hard to follow, and there are few other landmarks in this area. The most notable features of the Frog Level area are the wide meadows along Laurel Fork and the intersecting creek from the parking area. Those planning to hike from this access should take note of the junctions for their return, for they are easily overlooked when walking along the main Laurel Fork Trail route.

Access 5: Laurel Fork Trail from Cherry Flats Area

Atop the ridge from Dennis Cove, the turn to Frog Level in Access 4, continue straight on the main USFS-50 for another 3.2 miles to a three way intersection with USFS-39. The left branch, Little Stoney Road, leads back to US-321 in 5.1 miles, intersecting the highway one mile northeast of the Watauga Point Recreation Area. To reach the Cherry Flats Access, turn right along Walnut Mountain Road, and USFS-50-A is reached in 3.8 miles.

Route 50-A is noted on a small metal post for the single track, gravel road. A right turn at this junction leads one mile to a turnaround with limited parking.

There are two gates at this dead end. The closed road which continues straight ahead and due west from the gate leads 0.5 mile to the first ford of Laurel Fork Creek and its trail. Downstream from this point the **Laurel Fork Trail** follows an old railroad bed for an estimated 9 miles to the Dennis Cove Campground, passing through Frog Level en route (Access 3 and 4).

Connections with the Appalachian Trail:

1) From the first ford above, walk downstream on the Laurel Fork Trail for approximately 100 yards; turn left onto a wide, clearly defined path, and walk another 100 yards to a gravel logging road. Turn left and walk about one mile to where the white painted blazes will be noted on either side of the road.

2) For an all-day circuit (at least 15 miles), the Laurel Fork Trail can be followed to Dennis Cove Road and the Appalachian Trail back, along White Rocks Mountain (also see Access 2 and the Appalachian Trail section).

3) Continuing from the junction of USFS-50-A along Walnut Mountain Road: Note your mileage at this point, since there are no landmarks and the white trail blazes are very difficult to spot traveling along the roadway. The Appalachian Trail crosses the road at 1.5 miles from USFS-50-A.

Access 6: Cherry Flats/Walnut Mountain Road from U.S. 19-E/Roan Mountain area

Access points 2, 3, 4 and 5 can also be approached from the opposite direction, from U.S. 19-E, near the town of Roan Mountain. From the junction of Routes 143/19-E, travel 1.5 miles on 19-E toward North Carolina, and turn left beside the Roan Mountain Animal Hospital. Bear right, up the mountain, and the paved Walnut Mountain Road turns left at 3.5 miles from the highway. The road passes Laurel Fork Church, turns to gravel, and reaches the Appalachian Trail in 1.5 miles. The Route 50-A turn to Cherry Flats, to the Laurel Fork Trail, is another 1.5 miles.

Pond Mountain Area

Pond Mountain Trail
Trail distance: 5 miles, estimated, one way.
Difficulty rating: Difficult.

The Pond Mountain Trail is a high woodland walk which begins near Watauga Lake and rises to 4,329 feet on the crest. The route is poorly defined and better suited to the more adventurous. As mountaineers say, "It's as steep as a mule's face" coming up from Watauga Lake, with an altitude gain of about 1,800 feet in the first 1.5 miles. The walk is slightly easier from the USFS-50 end, since the hike begins higher on the mountain. Most of the walk is within the Pond Mountain Wilderness Area, which is rebounding as a bear habitat. It also has a large deer population, in addition to abundant smaller animals, fowl, and reptiles. The trail is around 5 miles of mostly difficult walking. There are screened views atop the summit and primitive connections with the Appalachian Trail can be found near the Pond Flats area.

There is another Pond Mountain (many names in the region are repeated) on the Virginia/North Carolina border in the Mount Rogers area. It is not included in this guidebook.

How to Get There

Access 1: Watauga Lake area.

Map for this area is on page 194.

From the US-321/19-E junction at Hampton, drive east toward Boone on US-321; the Watauga Point Recreation area is on the left in 6 miles. The walk can be started directly across the highway at the orange Forest Service Gate.

Access 2: Dennis Cove area on USFS Route 50.

From the Hampton turn (above), turn right onto Dennis Cove Road at 0.8 mile, beside the Citizens Bank; pass the Appalachian Trail (at 4.1 miles) and

Dennis Cove Recreation area (at 5 miles); continue for 2 more miles on a steep gravel road to the summit. At the top of the mountain, USFS-50-F turns right to Frog Level; the closed left fork, USFS-50-E, is the trail head.

This point can also be reached from the other end by continuing east beyond the Watauga Point Recreation area (Access 1) on US-321, for one mile. Turn right onto Little Stoney Road (USFS-39) and at 5.1 miles turn right again, onto USFS-50. The USFS-50-E/50-F intersection is 3.2 miles away.

Another trail head worth noting en route is the **Little Pond Mountain Trail**. It turns northward from the graveled Little Stoney Road at the crest of the route up from Watauga Lake.

Watauga Lake at Watauga Point, the terminus of the Pond Mountain Trail.

The Trail

The Pond Mountain Trail, from the Watauga Point area, is initially up a power line road and right-of-way. Good views of the lake are offered from the swath. At the ridge shoulder an old road leads downhill to points near the lake and Little Stoney Road. The largest of these tracks also turns up the ridge spur, and faded yellow blazes may still be found. The trail is soon reduced to a faint path with occasional yellow ribbons marking the primitive hunting track. The route is mostly to the south along the summit.

The peak is reached at about 3½ miles from Watauga Lake. Below the peak, the trail descends along the eastern shoulder of the mountain to closed Route 50-E. Route 50-E turns west around the contour of the mountain to intersect the **Bear Stand Trail**, which connects with the **Appalachian Trail**, or goes south to Access 2.

To begin the walk at the USFS-50/50-E point (where there is a vertical metal marker for 50-E, hiker-only notices, and large parking area), it is helpful to become familiar with the landmarks visible from the gap. Due to recent clear cuts in the area, there are relatively open views. Closed Route 50-E can be picked out where it travels from this ridge along the contours of Pond Mountain. The Pond Mountain Trail turns right from Route 50-E in about one mile, at a sharp bend of the road beside a small spring branch. Continuing along this road in a more westerly direction, the Bear Stand Trail turns left from the lane by a primitive unmarked path that is rapidly becoming choked by briars.

Bear Stand Trail

The Bear Stand Trail is rapidly being reclaimed by nature. It turns from the Appalachian Trail above the Pond Flats Shelter to climb to the Bear Stand overlook on the crest of Pond Mountain. It is a primitive path passable only in winter. It can also be approached from closed USFS-50-E as above. Unless it gets either more maintenance or traffic to beat down the undergrowth, it is recommended only for trail blazers.

Little Pond Mountain Trail

The Little Pond Mountain trail connects Little Stoney Road to US-321 in the Little Milligan area. It is in the 5 mile range. I have only walked the couple of miles in the summit area, where it is a wide, moderately easy walk. It has no blazes or signs, but receives trail bike use and is easily followed. From the Little Stoney Road, about ¾ mile from the USFS-39/50 junction, the trail leads nearly straight north. There are several forest roads and biker tracks in the area.

Iron Mountain Area

Appalachian Trail/Iron Mountain Trail
North From Watauga Dam Road to Holston Mountain
Trail segment distance: 15.6 miles, one way.
Difficulty rating: Moderate, north bound; Easy, south bound.

Map for this area is on page 194.

The Iron Mountain Trail is the second longest footpath in this region. It extends, with numerous connections, from the Watauga Lake area in Tennessee to VA-94 near Fries, Virginia. Most of the route is between 3,000 and 4,000 feet; it ranges from a primitive, rough path to wide, easily traversed thoroughfares. This trail is at its best in the Mount Rogers National Recreation Area (from Damascus to near Troutdale) and when combined with the Appalachian Trail, as it is for most of this segment. Throughout its more than 60 miles it offers varied terrain and has scenery ranging from deep hardwood forests to spectacular panoramas. Numerous circuit routes lasting for a couple of hours to several days can be planned including the Iron Mountain Trail.

The Appalachian/Iron Mountain Trail in this segment is a long uninterrupted walk along the spine of Iron Mountain. There are good views and unusual geology exposed in the rocky cliffs and sharp tops along the way.

Access 1: Watauga Dam Road

From US-321/19-E, traveling toward Roan Mountain at Elizabethton, turn onto Siam Road and follow TVA signs to Watauga Dam. Also, there is a TVA sign directing to the dam from US-321/19-E at Valley Forge. The Appalachian Trail blazes are visible on the hillcrest before reaching the visitor center and parking lot.

This access may also be reached from TN-91. Siam Road is a right turn beside Citizens Bank, and there is a TVA sign to the dam at 3.5 miles north of the US-321/19-E/TN-91 junction. **Note that this mileage may be off by**

a couple of tenths of a mile due to new U.S. 19-E construction at Elizabethton.

An alternate, very primitive route for the Iron Mountain Trail begins in the Blue Springs Community and climbs the northwestern slope of the mountain. It intersects the Appalachian Trail on the summit, about two miles from the dam road. Blue Springs Road turns from Siam Road on the TN-91 side of the river. In the vicinity of Wilson's Grocery, a couple of country lanes turn toward the foot of the mountain, and the primitive connector paths can be found entering the Forest Service boundary near their ends. It may be necessary to have them pointed out since they are very obscure.

Access 2: Tennessee Route 91 near Carter/Johnson County line.

Map for this area is on page 195.

From the Elizabethton US-321/19-E/TN-91 junction, drive north for 19 miles. En route, the Cherokee National Forest (Watauga District) Ranger Station is passed at 1.2 miles from the junction; it is a good source of maps and trail condition updates. The Appalachian Trail crossing is noted near the Johnson/Carter County lines, but there is no parking here and it is in a dangerous curve. Drive another 0.2 mile, and paved USFS-53/Doe Valley Road turns right, where there is off-road parking. The turn is at the green 21 mile post. Walk back along the highway shoulder to the white blazed route.

Two alternate starting points for both the Appalachian and Iron Mountain Trails turn from the Doe Valley Road. At 0.4 mile from the highway, closed USFS-60551 turns right. There is a metal post marker and gate. The Appalachian Trail is about 100 feet along this grass seeded road. Continuing along Doe Valley Road to a point one mile from TN-91, an old road turns right into the woods and reaches the Appalachian Trail in about ½ mile. This path is still frequently used.

Just ahead on the right side of Doe Valley Road is a new microwave antenna installation, at 1.1 miles from TN-91. Directly across the pavement, a rough single track turns diagonally into the woods along the hill crest. At 350 yards from the pavement, Wildlife Management Area notices and U.S. Forest Service boundary markers are crossed. Yellow painted blazes on trees flank the old road at this point and mark the continuing northward route of the Iron Mountain Trail.

These points can also be reached from TN-67 (located between Hampton and Mountain City), by turning onto the paved road beside the Doe Valley Methodist Church. Continue up the mountain, and the antenna compound is reached in 4.7 miles.

The Trail

Beginning from the Watauga Dam Road at the southern end of the segment, the Appalachian and Iron Mountain Trails follow the same course. The single file footpath is well maintained and marked, although it is not one of the more heavily traveled links on the Georgia to Maine trek. In this section it treads along the sharp spine of Iron Mountain, running nearly constantly to the northeast. The path probably predates the Appalachian Trail, since it has been popular with hunters for generations. Occasional hunters may be encountered in the area during the different seasons since the woods support a varied wildlife population including deer, turkey, and grouse as large as domestic chickens. Part of this segment is through a recently designated Wilderness Area.

North from Watauga Dam Road, the trail has a steady, moderate grade for about the first mile. Down the ridge to the right are glimpses of Watauga Lake, and to the left Holston Mountain, running parallel.

The walking is easier once you are atop the crest and rocky outcrops offer a bit more scenery with trees framing the vistas. Since the lake is over 1,000 feet below at this point, sailboats look like toys. The marinas and other landmarks along the shore are easily picked out. Looking toward the area beyond the lake, Pond Mountain and its lower ridges are found where the Appalachian Trail's route winds south through Laurel Fork and Dennis Cove, to White Rocks Mountain and beyond.

The path continues along the narrow crest, with the lake side particularly steep, ranging from greater than forty-five degrees to vertical. Grades on the other side are not quite as severe, but abrupt enough to keep the hiker on the blazed course.

The primitive Iron Mountain Trail approach from the Blue Springs area intersects the marked path at around 2 miles. It is a partly overgrown, unmarked timber road coming in at one of the wider flats atop the summit. There are other rough side paths or old jeep roads approaching the summit at the gaps, but they are steep spurs down to the Stoney Creek or Butler areas.

The forest is mixed hardwoods, with occasional scrubby pines and fairly large groves of hemlock. In autumn the emerald evergreen boughs look as if they are decorated for Christmas, with brilliant reds and yellows of maple and dogwood leaves sparkling in the filtered sunlight.

A point of interest atop the ridge crest: at 12.4 miles is the grave of hermit Nick Grindstaff, who spent most of his life in the vicinity. His eight-foot high monument, built of mortar and native stones, has a cracked marble plaque with this poignant inscription:

"Uncle Nick Grindstaff—born Dec.26, 1851—died July 22, 1923—lived alone, suffered alone, died alone."

The marker now stands very much alone on the high, windy ridge near the trail's west side. The nearest road is more than three miles away, at the TN-91 or Doe Valley Road accesses.

Approximate distances from Watauga Dam Road are: Vandevinter Shelter, 4.5 miles; Iron Mountain Shelter, 11.1 miles; Iron Mountain Trail diversion to Doe Valley Road, 14.4; intersect TN-91, 15.6 miles.

From the Highway 91 intersection, the Appalachian Trail crosses to the shoulder of Holston Mountain. The Iron Mountain Trail continues along the crest of Iron Mountain, skirting private holdings and heavy timbering in the area to follow a route nearly parallel to the white marked trail to Damascus.

Iron Mountain Trail

Continuing North From Doe Valley Road to Damascus, Virginia.
Trail segment distance: 18 miles, estimated, one way.
Difficulty rating: Mostly moderate, but with Difficult sections where *Br'er Rabbit* would have to pack a lunch.

Map for this area is on page 196.

The Doe Valley Road (USFS-53) approach to the Iron Mountain Trail is included in Access 2 of the Appalachian Trail/Iron Mountain segment. The trail south turns to the right at one mile along paved Doe Valley Road (USFS-53), from TN-91. It follows an old road about ½ mile to intersect the Appalachian Trail. The route north turns left from Doe Valley Road, just beyond the turn south, along a rough off-road vehicle track. This road running diagonally along the hill is directly across from a new microwave antennae installation. Yellow painted blazes and Forest Service boundary notices are reached in 350 yards. The blazes continue along the summit by the old road.

Parts of the path in this link deteriorate to near primitive with rare markings for wayfarers. Other sections get used by hunters (the main users of this area), trail bikes and horses. There are occasional diamond trail markers and faded paint blazes to reassure the hiker. The route keeps to the high ground, offering occasional peeps through the trees at the small farmsteads lying below in the folds of an infinity of mountains. Sections of logging clear cuts are also viewed along this route.

Hardwoods grow amid the boulders above Watauga Dam, along the Appalachian Trail on Iron Mountain.

Trail distance from USFS-53 to the crossing of US-421 is roughly 5 miles.

Iron Mountain Trail: Continuing northeast from U.S. 421 to near Damascus.

Traveling north from this access, you will find that the Iron Mountain Trail offers 12 to 13 miles of uninterrupted hiking along the mountain crest that rises to over 4,000 feet. The south side of the highway has a three foot high post to mark the trail head. On the north side of the highway there is a wooden plaque, just up the hill from steps set into the road embankment. Parking is along the highway shoulder.

By road this point is 4.2 miles toward Mountain City from the TN-91/US-421 junction at Shady Valley.

There are hiker-only notices at both the north and south heads of the trail. Both segments are rarely used except by hunters in the fall and winter seasons. Recent maintenance has renewed many of the trail blazes and removed dead falls. The route north from the U.S. 421 crossing begins well marked with yellow painted blazes and is well defined. There is a gradual climb from U.S. 421 to the peak of Grindstone Knob; then the path follows the slowly undulating crest over a trail that is rated moderate. Rough logging and other closed forest roads descend the ridges at gaps and ridge flats, the first one (descending Lewis Ridge) being encountered in less than a mile at a small clearing. The next major track is about 4 miles and it departs to the northwest (following Birch Branch) to Route-133 in the valley.

There are fallen trees across the trail at several points and occasional detours may be required, but in general the trail keeps to the spine of the mountain. The next major tracks from the summit are reached in about 2.5 miles. They descend along Camp Hollow and Tank Hollow to Route 133 and to the newly graveled logging access road USFS-300, which emerges from the woods near the Backbone Rock area.

Continuing on the Iron Mountain crest, this less-used area is more difficult going, although the path is fairly well defined. An old road which once connected the Sutherland and Laurel Bloomery areas across the mountain is reached at about 8 to 9 miles from the U.S. 421 access. It turns off both sides of the crest. The Corinth Church is roughly one mile down the southern slope, and the Sutherland community (down the north slope) is about 3 miles away.

From this junction, the trail continues for another 2 miles or so to the Butt Mountain peak. After beginning the descent, branches in the path lead off in the directions of the Methodist Camp, and by a more primitive path, to a secondary road near Damascus. Until this junction is reached, the route is nearly straight to the northeast from the crossing at U.S. 421.

The Damascus base of the mountain in this link is broad and steep. Exploring, detours, and bushwhacking may be expected to join or leave the Iron Mountain Trail from this butt of the mountain.

Road access points for this section are from TN-133/VA-716 and Highway 91. These state routes travel parallel valleys along Iron Mountain, between Shady Valley on the north side, or Mountain City on the south, to Damascus.

Route 133 Access points:

At 6.5 miles from the Shady Valley crossroads, Birch Branch is crossed. Camp Hollow Creek turns just beyond the 8 mile post, and Tank Hollow Creek (USFS-300) turns near the 9 mile post. With the exception of Birch Branch, these closed forest roads travel to turnarounds or connections along the lower ridge contours, but end before reaching the summit. Secondary paths skirt the thickets and briars from clear cuts to climb to the summit. The Backbone Rock Recreation Area is 9.5 miles. The old road over the mountain (USFS-322) can be located by turning onto timber road 6044, beyond the tunnel and picnic area. Turn left at about ½ mile, toward the power line right-of-way. The old road is to the east of the power lines and is still fairly clear.

TN-133 becomes VA-716 at the Virginia line. Sugarcamp Branch, ½ mile beyond the state line, can also be followed up the mountain. This and most of the routes up the mountain begin easily enough, but deteriorate to difficult, with briars, undergrowth, fallen trees and uncertain paths before reaching the Iron Mountain Trail on the crest.

Route 91 Access points:

Signs to the Deer Run development are at 6.5 miles north from Mountain City. Turn left and the Corinth Church is reached in 1.5 miles. Directly across from the church parking lot there is a rough lane heading toward the top of the mountain. This is the old Route 322 to the Sutherland and Backbone Rock areas. The Forest Service right-of-way can be followed to the trail atop the mountain, although the lands on either side are posted with no trespassing notices. The mountain can also be climbed from within the National Forest boundary located at 1.5 miles (left from the church along the gravel road), but this is a more difficult route.

An old farmstead near the Iron Mountain Trail access in the Laurel Bloomery area.

The Iron Mountain Trail reaches Highway 91 at the Methodist Camp A-Hi-S-Ta-Di, or again at 0.3 mile from Route 91, on Route 1212 near Damascus.

Gentry Creek Trail and Waterfall
Trail distance: 2.5 miles, one way estimated.
Difficulty rating: Moderate.

The Gentry Creek Trail is a pleasant creek side walk to a double waterfall near Laurel Bloomery, Tennessee. There are no trail blazes or signs, but most of the route is reasonably clear. The path is rarely used except by hunters or anglers. Much of the route is over abandoned rail or logging roadbeds, with little climbing, but laurel thickets threaten to take over parts of the course, and flooding has obliterated the track in places.

The waterfalls carry a fairly large volume of water. Both steps of the falls are in the 30 to 40 feet range, with small pools below them. Viewed together, they are more than impressive enough to justify the estimated 2.5 mile walk. Adjoining primitive trails also offer the opportunity to explore the surrounding ridges.

How to Get There

The Gentry Creek area is reached from TN-91, between Damascus, Virginia, and Mountain City, Tennessee. From Damascus, turn left at 6 miles from the US-58/91 South junction; from Mountain City, the turn is right at about 7.5 miles from the US-421 junction.

The turn is southeast at the A-Z Market and BP Station at Laurel Bloomery. There is a sign to Pleasant Home Church. From TN-91, drive 0.8 mile and turn right at the first intersection. The lane turns to gravel in 1.1 mile, at the National Forest boundary. Continue on the Forest Service track for another 1.4 miles. Parking is a wide spot near the creek that will accommodate a few cars. The single track gravel lane is passable by most cars, but the track continuing to the right, up the ridge, is best left to all-terrain machines and horses. The trail to the falls starts beyond the earthen mound barriers near the parking area.

The Trail

A small creek is forded at just under 100 yards from the mound barriers at the start of the walk, and in another 100 yards a fork in the trail is reached. Either branch can be followed.

The fork continuing straight ahead sticks closer to the creek. Part of this

A winter view of the double waterfalls on the Gentry Creek Trail.

route is swampy and has detours through thickets as well as additional wading. A plus for the creek side option is that it is easier to spot the correct branch of the stream leading to the falls. This is not a marked trail, and there are few landmarks to distinguish the turns.

The right fork is along the ridge shoulder. The grade falls within the easy category, and is followed for about ½ mile. It is wide, well defined and nearly level, since it is an old railroad bed. The stream through the gorge to the left can be seen and heard about 100 yards across the hollow. As the gorge narrows, close attention should be paid to the stream below and the ridges ahead, to spot the fork turning toward the falls. The main branch of the stream is to the left and flows from the northeast. This important branch can easily be overlooked, or the view screened from hikers along the ridge high road. I had hiked to the falls a few years ago, and I still missed this turn on my first attempt during a recent walk. Nearing the stream divide, climb down the slope as the roadbed turns more to the east; or, at the fork of the roadbed, descend left to the branch and work back downstream for a short distance to the main fork. There are several bearing trees and boundary markers near this junction, with red painted bands around the trees.

Should the turn be missed, the walk is also a pleasant one for a ways up a tumbling stream, but it becomes nearly impassable in about three miles. There are no falls.

From the fork to the waterfalls, follow old rutted tracks through the hollow upstream, generally to the north and northeast. Portions of the route may require minor detours due to undergrowth or washing out of the road, but it is fairly easy walking and the pathway is clearly visible near the stream bed. There are several creek crossings, but at wide spots with stepping stones.

Walking at a steady, unrushed pace, the first waterfall should be reached in around 1.5 hours. From this basin the second falls can be seen, directly above the first. To reach the upper falls, the rocks on the right side of the stream form a natural staircase up the wall. If you take this route, laurel growth presents a greater obstacle to reaching the second level than does the cliff; the undergrowth is so intertwined that it's almost as effective as a chain link fence in halting progress. However, by crawling over, around and through, the upper pool can be gained. (It becomes clear, in trying to pass through these thickets, why they were called "Laurel Hells" on the frontier.)

This trail could easily deteriorate to the difficult category, from lack of use and maintenance. It is not recommended during rainy periods or later in the growing season due to weed growth.

Holston Mountain Area

Appalachian Trail

North From Tennessee Highway 91 to U.S. 421 and Damascus, Virginia.

Trail segment distance: 21.5 miles, one way.

Difficulty rating: Moderate.

Connecting Trails: Iron Mountain, Holston Mountain, Backbone Rock Trails and others.

This segment of the Appalachian Trail is primarily along the crest of Holston Mountain. There are moderately graded climbs from the road access points, but in-between there are no major altitude changes, placing the walk along the crest within the easy stroll category.

Most of this link is around the 4,000 feet level, through mature native hardwood forest. There are screened views of valley farmsteads and of South Holston Lake, but the main feature is the high woodland.

The three main road approaches to the Appalachian Trail are on TN-91, US-421, and from downtown Damascus. Secondary accesses are from USFS-69 in the McQueen Gap area or from connecting trails (see Holston Mountain and Backbone Rock Trails).

How to Get There

Maps for this area are on pages 195 and 196.

Access 1: Tennessee Highway 91 on Cross Mountain.

The Appalachian Trail crosses TN-91 on Cross Mountain, connecting the Iron Mountain and Holston Mountain segments. This point is 19 miles northeast of the TN-91/US-321/19-E junction at Elizabethton, or 3.7 miles southwest of the TN-91/US-421 junction at Shady Valley. The trail sign and blazes are visible along the highway, but this is in a very dangerous curve. Off-road parking is at the top of the hill beside the turn of Doe Valley Road, near a green D.O.T. 21 mile post.

Access 2: U.S. 421, at Low Gap.

Off road parking, signs and visible white blazes mark the Appalachian Trail crossing at the crest of Holston Mountain on US-421. This is 2.8 miles west from the TN-91/US-421 junction at Shady Valley, or approximately 18 miles east of Bristol.

Access 3: Damascus, Virginia.

The Maine to Georgia trail travels through the main business district of Damascus. It is a major resupply and layover point for through hikers. A trail registry is maintained at the Post Office. Entering town on US-58 from the west, there is a sign noting the Appalachian Trail where the highway makes a sharp turn to cross Beaverdam Creek. South on the trail is straight ahead along Beaverdam Street for 0.3 mile; it turns onto Rural Street, and in the next block it heads up the hillside, between side yards of the residential street.

The trail head north is on the east side of Damascus on US-58, just before the junction of Highway 91 south.

Access 4: Backbone Rock Trail Connector.

The Backbone Rock Recreation Area can be reached by turning southwest onto VA-716 at its Damascus junction with US-58. Backbone Rock is 3.8 miles. The marked **Backbone Rock Trail** departs from the rock formation for a difficult 2 mile climb to the white blazed route.

This point may also be approached from Shady Valley on TN-133, 9.8 miles from the US-421 junction.

Access 5: McQueen Knob Road/USFS-69.

Rough USFS-69 crosses McQueen Gap and the Appalachian Trail at 3.2 miles from TN-133. The road turns up the mountain at 6.8 miles from the tunnel through Backbone Rock. Approached from Shady Valley, USFS-69 turns left from TN-133, 3 miles from the US-421/TN-133 junction.

An alternate route to McQueen Knob Road from the north side of the mountain follows Jacobs Creek Road from US-421 (it turns northeast 4 miles east of the bridge over South Holston Lake). This winding, paved road runs for 9.5 miles, passing Jacob's Creek Job Corps Center en route before becoming a single track forest road with turnouts. At 13.7 miles there is a four-way intersection, and a wooden marker indicates Route 69 on the right prong. At 17.2 miles white trail blazes are visible on orange gates on each side of the gap.

The Appalachian Trail: TN-91 to US-421.

Beginning at the TN-91 access on the Carter/Johnson County line, the Appalachian Trail travels along Cross Mountain between Iron and Holston Mountains. There are low ridges, small streams, and swampy areas for the first couple of miles, then a fairly long grade climbing Rich Knob. The Double Springs Shelter is reached in about 3.5 miles, and the intersecting **Holston Mountain Trail** also approaches the clearing from the southwest.

The shelter is a good place to take a break on day hikes. There is a comfortable lawn chair and trail log, thoughtfully left by a hiker; the log provides interesting reading. It is a spiral notebook, and contains entries from numerous overnight guests. They give updates on conditions along the route, and tell of their experiences on their treks. Part of the text is like snooping through someone's pen pal letters, but other writers express their favorite philosophies or try to entertain subsequent wayfarers around the campfire. One writer commented that he thought every shelter should have its own colony of wildcats nearby to wake hikers in the middle of the night with terrifying screams.

From the shelter it is less than 100 yards to the junction of **Holston Mountain Trail**. Marked with blue painted blazes on this end, it is rated moderate in difficulty and follows the ridge tops of Holston Mountain southwest to the Holston High Knob fire tower. The distance to the tower and gravel lane atop the mountain is 7.8 miles. The Holston Mountain Trail is not heavily used, but it is fairly well marked and maintained.

Skirting the Rich Knob peak, the Appalachian Trail returns to a generally northeastern direction. The remaining 3.4 miles to US-421 is mostly easy walking, since much of the path is gently downward. At an altitude of 4,247 feet, the north side of Rich Knob is covered with a lush green layer of moss, ferns and lichens, characteristic growth of deep woods where sunlight reaching the forest floor is diffused, and giant decaying logs support a varied flora.

There are occasional glimpses of South Holston Lake along the way, but none to compare with the view from the fire tower at the terminus of the **Holston Mountain Trail**. The thick canopy and under story screen the vistas to the west. The right side of the trail edges along private lands. Some of the abandoned pastures are still open enough to give splendid views of the pastoral countryside along Shady Valley, with its rolling farmlands and tidy buildings.

An old split rail fence, along the Appalachian Trail on Holston Mountain.

On the ridges separating the public and private lands there are remains of an old split rail fence. Made of rived chestnut, the nearly extinct monarchs of the Appalachian forest, the fence is probably 50-100 years old. In this age of machines, it represents the inconceivable amount of toil required to wrest pasture and field from the alpine ridges. Great piles of stone also line the boundaries, reminding today's traveler that not so long ago many of these rocky highlands were tilled for corn, wheat and other crops.

Near these fields a secondary blue blazed trail leaves the mountain toward water. The route is very steep, but the creek can be followed down the mountain to the abandoned site of Camp Tom Howard and USFS-87 along South Holston Lake.

This Appalachian Trail link from TN-91 to US-421 is 6.9 miles.

Appalachian Trail: Continuing north from U.S. 421.

From Low Gap at US-421, the footpath resumes its pattern of moderate grades, and the walking is easy along ridge flats. Most of this area is National Forest, and the trail is fairly well marked and maintained. There is substantially more climbing on the reverse route coming from the Damascus end. Most of the views are of the forest.

A fire tower, known as C-1, once stood atop McQueen Knob at 3,885 feet. All that remains is its foundation, which is passed at 3.3 miles. During the growing season the trail here is lined with briars and stinging nettles, and according to the journal at the Abingdon Gap Shelter, rattlesnakes are also prevalent. The old tower has been completely removed except for the concrete pads that supported its frame. (Airplanes are now used to spot wildfire, elminating the need to staff numerous such towers that once dotted the highlands.) An old privy lies on its side, along with utility poles that once connected the knob with the outside world. A forest road descends to Route 69 in about ½ mile.

Appalachian Trail: Continuing north from McQueen Gap.

Beyond USFS-69 (also called McQueen Knob Road), much of the trail follows closed and mostly reclaimed forest roads, making the grades gradual and the path fairly wide. The Abingdon Gap shelter is reached in 20-30 minutes of steady, unrushed walking. At the shelter, another spiral bound notebook which serves as a log contains entries from many of the same hikers writing in the Double Springs Shelter's journal. Here the accounts turn from the wildcats and wild strawberries of the Rich Knob stop over to sightings of deer, setting traps for mice, and stories of Paul's meeting the Savior on a pathway to the ancient capital of Syria. Damascus is only 16 kilometers ahead.

Most of this segment is unbroken by civilization, but there are trails leading off both sides of the mountain. One in particular, the blue blazed **Backbone Rock Trail**, heads east off the mountain at about 5.4 miles beyond the Abingdon Gap Shelter. It descends 2 miles to the odd geological formation of Backbone Rock and a splendid little waterfall at the Backbone Rock Recreation Area, located on TN-133 and Beaverdam Creek. The Virginia/Tennessee state line is reached in another 0.7 mile along the white marked path. Damascus is about 4 miles from the Backbone Rock Trail junction.

The distance from US-421 to Damascus is 14.5 miles by the Appalachian Trail.

Summer time at the Blue Hole on Holston Mountain.

Backbone Rock Area

Map for this area is on page 196.

Backbone Rock is, as the name implies, an unusual geological formation resembling a great stony spine in the valley between Holston and Iron Mountains. TN-133 tunnels through the rock wall in northwest Johnson County, Tennessee, between Shady Valley and Damascus. The adjacent recreation area offers camping and picnic facilities, and is popular on weekends.

The rock spine can be climbed by steps set into the side of the formation.

There is a lovely small waterfall near the rock, and a short trail makes a loop past it from the parking area. There are short nature trails along Beaverdam Creek within the recreation area. The **Backbone Rock Trail** connects with the **Appalachian Trail** atop Holston Mountain, and unmarked paths lead up the Iron Mountain slopes to the **Iron Mountain Trail** (see Iron Mountain Trail section).

Backbone Rock is on TN-133. From Shady Valley, at the TN-133/US-421 junction, there is a sign pointing to the recreation area, which is reached in about 9.5 miles.

From Damascus, take VA-716 south from US-58 in the middle of the business district. There is a sign at this junction, and the tunnel through Backbone Rock is 3.7 miles.

Waterfall Loop Trail

The loop trail to the small waterfall is from the southwest side of the roadway, on the Shady Valley side of the tunnel. Rock steps lead along the small stream at about 100 yards from the parking. A sign warns parents to watch their children.

The falls are only another 100 yards or so from the pavement. Continuing beyond the falls, the path climbs to above the ribbon of water, crosses the creek to a small overlook, then descends back to the parking area. The total distance of the falls loop is around ¼ mile of well traveled path.

From the parking lot on the northwest side of TN-133, there is a paved

Waterfall at the Backbone Rock Recreation Area, reached by short path.

nature trail along Beaverdam Creek, but the main attraction here is the vertical face of Backbone Rock. Concrete and stone steps ascend to the top of the spine, and a walkway with handrails crosses the arch above the highway. Stairways also scale the rock from the picnic/camping area.

Backbone Rock Trail

Trail distance: 2 miles, one way to Appalachian Trail.
Difficulty rating: difficult, due to strenuous climb.

The Backbone Rock Trail, which connects TN-133 with the **Appalachian Trail** atop Holston Mountain, departs from the northwestern end of the rock. As the steps from the parking lot near the top of the rock end, the less-traveled Backbone Rock Trail turns left, up the ridge.

Blue painted blazes mark the route, but many of these are small patches and faded. The path is a distinct, single file course through the trees; the slope is not especially steep, but it is relentless.

There are few level breathers in the uphill struggle of just over 2 miles. Mostly one just hangs to the trees and gasps. From the junction with the white blazed route, Damascus (at about 4 miles), Mount Rogers, and points north lie to the right. The southern route winds along the crest of the mountain, with the first break in the trail occuring at USFS-69 at McQueen Gap, about 6.7 miles.

Holston Mountain Trail

Trail distance: 7.8 miles, one way.
Difficulty rating: Moderate.
Connections: Appalachian, Flint Mill and Josiah Creek Trails.

The Holston Mountain Trail is a pleasant woodland walk. Beginning at the Holston High Knob fire tower, the course is marked and fairly easy walking. Except through the gaps, the grades are gradual. The footpath is fairly well maintained, although heavy summer growth may partly obscure the path. There are splendid views from the tower and from rocky outcrops in the Flint Mill Gap area. The trail terminus is at the Double Springs Shelter intersection with the Appalachian Trail, approximately 7.8 miles northeast.

How to Get There

Maps for this area are on pages 194 and 195.

To reach Holston High Knob fire tower, drive 10.6 miles northeast on TN-91 from the TN-91/US-321/19-E junction at Elizabethton. (Note a potential slight mileage variation due to current US-19-E interchange construction.) Turn left up Holston Mountain onto Panhandle Road; there is a sign at the intersection. The fire tower is visible from TN-91 in this area. The paved lane turns to a gravel, all-weather Forest Service road in one mile.

View from the fire tower near the beginning of the Holston Mountain Trail.

A picturesque detour is possible here: Just beyond the end of the blacktop there is a turnout parking area on the left, with a path leading to the "Blue Hole," a series of small waterfalls and pools. It is a favorite area swimming hole in warm weather. The distance to the creek is only about 100 yards and it is a short walk downstream to the falls.

Continuing up the mountain, the road is a single track with turnouts and reaches the juncture of USFS-202/56-A at the top, 4.5 miles from TN-91. Turn right here and bear right, keeping to the more heavily traveled lane; the tower is one mile. A new gate has been added at about ¼ mile from

A small waterfall at the Blue Hole area of Holston Mountain.

the above junction restricting motorized traffic to the tower; effectively adding ¾ mile to the walk.

The trail heads northeast from the last bend of the road, about 100 yards from the base of the tower. There is a hiking trail sign nailed to a tree, and a three-foot high post which identifies the Holston Mountain Trail.

The trail can be approached from other trails in the area, including: The Appalachian Trail (see TN-91 and US-421 access points), and the Flint Mill and Josiah Creek Trails (see separate trail entries).

The Holston Mountain Trail: North from the Holston High Knob Fire Tower.

Before beginning this walk, a climb up part of the fire tower will yield an excellent view of the Holston Mountain Trail route, as well as of the South Holston Lake, all the area mountains, and the entire Tri/Quad-Cities area. Only six people are permitted on the structure at a time and anyone even slightly afraid of heights should avoid it. The tower is a popular excursion on clear weekends.

This trail would probably benefit from more hikers to beat the weeds down during the summer growing season, but the single file path is clearly defined throughout its distance, even fallen trees have had notches or steps cut into them for easy passage.

This was once the Appalachian Trail route and painted blazes have been retained. They vary in color from yellow and orange (on its southern end) to blue near the Appalachian Trail end.

Most of the walk is very pleasant and is especially easy near the tower end, as the path follows the gentle rise and fall of the crest. The forest is made up of mature hardwoods, and there are glimpses of the lake, the mountains, and the Stoney Creek valley along the summit. Excellent views of the lake can be had in the Flint Mill Gap area by taking the **Flint Mill Gap/Mountain Trail**. At the gap, about 2.5 miles from the tower, a fairly clear old road reaches the crest from the north side of the mountain.

The forest lane receives frequent horse traffic and turns west from the gap. This is the old **Flint Mill Gap Road**, and it descends steeply along a hollow and creek to the **Flatwoods Horse Trail**, near the lake.

A blue blazed footpath (marked with a sign **"Flint Mtn. Trail"**) also descends this side of the mountain passing Flint Rock about ½ mile from the gap. This hiker-only path turns northwest from the junction and is a relatively easy stroll along the plateau to the view from Flint Rock cliff. The route then drops very severely for its remaining mile to the **Flatwoods Horse**

Trail; then to USFS-87. The designated hiker trail received substantial work in 1991 and is clear and well marked.

Continuing northeast on the Holston Mountain Trail: The difficulty rating progresses to moderate at about the midway point and the intersection with the **Flatwoods/Josiah Creek Trails** (which lead off the north side of the mountain).

From the junction of the **Appalachian Trail** at the Double Springs Shelter, it is about 3.5 miles from the shelter to either US-421 (north on the white blazed route) or to TN-91.

Flint Mill Gap Trail
Trail distance: 1.5 miles, one way.
Difficulty rating: Difficult, clear path but hard climb.

The **Flint Mill Gap Trail** climbs Holston Mountain from USFS-87/87-A near South Holston Lake. This difficult rated 1.5 mile climb up the north slope joins the **Holston Mountain Trail** at Flint Mill Gap, about 2.5 miles northeast from the fire tower.

View of South Holston Lake on the Flint Mill Gap Trail.

This foot trail has recently been upgraded with signs at both ends, newly painted blue blazes, and fallen trees and brush removed. En route, it crosses the **Flatwoods Trail Horse Trail** and an old road (which also climbs to the gap).

Attractions of the route include views from Flint Rock Cliffs (a 1 mile hard climb) and prolific wildflower displays in May and June along the ½ mile plateau (between the cliff and the Holston Mountain Trail), including mountain laurel, Catawba rhododendron, and pink lady slippers. It also makes an excellent connector for circuit hikes linking the Holston Mountain and Flatwoods Trails.

The trail head is noted with a sign beside USFS-87 at 3 miles northeast of the Hickory Tree Junction, or 3.7 miles southwest from the Little Oak Campground entrance.

Josiah Creek/Flatwoods Trail
Trail distance: 2.5 miles, one way.
Difficulty rating: Moderate, with steep sections.
Horse/Mountain Bike Use.

The **Josiah Creek Hiker Trail** turns south from USFS-87 at 1.4 miles southwest of the Little Oak Campground. Also used as a horse trail to the old Flatwoods Road (USFS-87-A), the route is a moderate climb of the north side of the mountain. It crosses Route 87-A about ½ mile from the trail head and reaches the crest and an intersection with the **Holston Mountain Trail** in around 2.5 miles. This junction is about midway between the fire tower and Rich Knob.

The **Josiah Horse Trail** begins 0.4 mile closer to the Little Oak turn. This route is slightly steeper and longer than the hiker route and intersects the **Flatwoods Trail** about ¾ mile from the trail head sign, a few hundred yards east of the hiker route.

Both routes have recently been upgraded with signs and clearing.

Holston Mountain Trail—
Southwest end of the Mountain

Horse/Mountain Bike Use.

This is an off-road vehicle track that can be hiked. It begins opposite the

Omnirange Navigation Beacon at Holston High Point (the "High Point" and "High Knob" are different places), 4.1 miles southwest on gravel USFS-202 from the 202/56-A intersection. This junction is listed above for the fire tower and northern link of the trail. There is a three-foot high post with **"Holston Mountain Trail"** routed into it. It is rated moderate in difficulty as a hiker route.

Approximately 2 miles from the trail head marker, another forest road turns left along the southern slope to Little Stoney Creek; then descends gradually for about 4 miles to TN-91, emerging from the woods onto the secondary road on the northeast side of Unaka High School. This is the old USFS-202 route.

Continuing southwest on the Holston Mountain Trail, the **Keener Spur Motorcycle Trail** is met in about a mile, and the **Big Barrett Trail** is another ½ mile. These two trail bike routes make a 5.5 mile loop from USFS-87. The Holston Mountain Trail continues along the southwest foot of the mountain for about 4 miles before terminating at Route 87, at the National Forest boundary near Keenburg Community. Distance from Holston High Point to the bottom of the mountain is estimated in the 8 mile range of moderately graded walking.

Other Holston Mountain Trails

Road Approaches to Holston Mountain Trails along USFS-87:

USFS-87 is a good all-weather road connecting US-421 and US-19-E. It follows the northwest base of Holston Mountain for about 25 miles, parallel with South Holston Lake. There is one major crossroads, Hickory Tree junction, where USFS-251 turns to the Hickory Tree community and TN-44.

Road distances to trail heads from US 19-E, traveling northeast.

A paved secondary road turns from U.S. 19-E at 3.2 miles from the U.S. 19-E/321 junction at Elizabethton (due to new interchange construction at Elizabethton a slight mileage variation may be noted). Distances noted are from the 4-lane:

1.5 miles: A gated/gravel timber access road turns southeast between private and public property. This road ends in about 3 miles and serves as one terminus of **Holston Mountain Trail** for hikers. It connects with four-wheel and ATV routes on the ridge spur, but this section is closed to vehicles.

2.0 miles, approximate: The National Forest boundary is noted; the road becomes gravel, and numerous unmarked ATV routes and closed timber roads connect with the winding lane from this point.

6.4 miles: The **Keener Spur Trail** head is marked by a sign; loading ramp and parking areas are provided. Confirming the route's difficulty someone has added to the ATV sign, "SOB."

11.0 miles: **Flatwoods Horse Trail**: It is a steep, narrow path at this end, but it connects with easy closed roads. There is a sign beside the road.

11.4 miles: The **Morrell Trail**, a blue blazed path marked by a sign, is 100 feet west of the power lines.

11.8 miles: Hickory Tree Junction where a left turn onto USFS-251 leads to TN-44 at Hickory Tree; the continuing route of USFS-87 is a right turn.

The following distances are from Hickory Tree Junction, continuing northeast on USFS-87: **Short Spur Trail** (marked with blue blazes and sign), 1.6 mile; **Flint Mill Gap Trail** (blue blazes and sign), 3 miles; **Josiah Hiker Trail** (blue blazes and sign), 5.3 miles; **Josiah Horse Trail** (horse trail sign) 5.7 miles; and Little Oak Campground entrance, 6.7 miles.

Trail Head Distances Along USFS-87 traveling Southwest, from US-421.

Traveling from Bristol on US-421, USFS-87 turns right at 3.5 miles from the South Holston Lake bridge. Distances from the highway are:

0.4 mile: Camp Tom Howard, an abandoned Boy Scout Camp, is noted with a native stone pillar. Unmarked, primitive footpaths lead from roadway up north slope of mountain.

1.0 mile: USFS-87-B, **Flatwoods Horse Trail** head.

6.8 miles: Little Oak Campground entrance road.

7.8 miles: **Josiah Horse Trail** trailhead (horse trail sign).

8.2 miles: **Josiah Hiker Trail** head (sign and blue blazes).

10.5 miles: **Flint Mill Gap Trail** head (sign and blue blazes).

12.1 miles: **Short Spur Trail** head (sign and blue blazes).

13.5 miles: Hickory Tree Road Junction.

Flatwoods Trail
Horse/Mountain Bike Use.

This designated horse trail follows closed timber roads USFS-87-A and 87-B for about 8.5 miles, then mountain trails for another 5.5 miles. It runs roughly parallel to USFS-87 and has several marked and unmarked connectors. The eastern end of the gated/gravel route begins at the closed gate for USFS-87-B, at 1 mile from the US-421/USFS-87 junction. The graded segment intersects Route 87 again at 0.2 mile west of Hickory Tree Road (on its western end). The mountain trail head for the route is another 0.6 mile west. There are good views at cleared wildlife meadows.

It is rated easy walking as it follows the lower, graded contours of the mountain. It connects with the **Flint Mill, Josiah Creek, Short Spur** and **Morrell Trails** that climb to the mountain crest.

Short Spur Trail

This blue blazed trail connects USFS-87 (near South Holston Lake), to USFS-202 on the crest of Holston Mountain. It is approximately 2 miles of moderate to difficult climbing.

From the bottom of the mountain, the trail begins at 1.4 miles east of the Hickory Tree Road junction. The route has recently been upgraded and has a sign at its trail head. The **Flatwoods Trail** is crossed en route.

Atop the mountain, the trail turns downhill just west of the power lines crossing the summit on USFS-202. This is 0.1 mile west of the 56-A/202 junction.

Morrell Trail

From the bottom of the mountain, the Morrell Trail begins on USFS-87 at 0.4 mile west of the Hickory Tree Road Junction. The route has recently had some upgrading with blue painted blazes and a vertical trail head sign.

It climbs the mountain along moderate to steep grades in about 2 miles. It connects with USFS-202 on the crest (midway between Holston Knob and Holston High Point); the **Flatwoods Trail** is crossed en route.

Keener Spur/Barrett Hollow Trail

The Keener Spur is a 5.5 mile motorcycle designated loop from Route 87. It travels southward up the mountain; joins the **Holston Mountain four wheel route** on the southwestern slope briefly; then descends via the Barrett Hollow route (northwestward) back to USFS-87. This foot of the mountain is laced with trail bike routes meeting the gravel road. Other loop options include the Big Arm and Lock Ridge tracks.

Trail Upgrading in the Watauga Ranger District

According to Pete Irvine, Cherokee National Forest ranger at Elizabethton, there is a growing emphasis on recreational trails in the Watauga Ranger District. This has resulted in substantial improvements to a number of area backcountry routes recently. Work is continuing on other paths.

The Watauga Ranger District office is located on TN-91, about a mile north of the U.S. 19-E intersection. It is an excellent source for current trail conditions and topographical maps.

The current trend toward improving trail maintenance and the addition of signs and blazes may continue in this area of the National Forest, as well as in the other districts, if sufficient public interest is demonstrated. There are numerous competing interests for limited U.S. Forest Service personnel and funds, and public input influences where these are used.

Double blazes mark a turn in the Appalachian Trail on Whitetop Mountain.

Mount Rogers National Recreation Area

Appalachian Trail: North from Damascus, Virginia.

Map for this area is on page 196.

This segment of the Appalachian Trail leads north from Damascus, Virginia, to the Mount Rogers National Recreation Area Headquarters and Visitors center, on Virginia Highway 16. The link traverses approximately 70 miles of the Maine to Georgia footpath and comprises the most diverse and beautiful trail segments in Virginia.

Lying totally inside the Mount Rogers National Recreation Area, the section presents numerous opportunities for connections with other trails within the reserve's network of well-maintained and marked footpaths. Most of these connecting paths are in the moderate and easy range of difficulty and can be linked for circuit walks of varying lengths. There are several good published maps of the Recreation Area; current conditions may be updated at the Visitors Center. In addition to the hiker trails, there are also systems of cross-country ski routes, horse trails, and motorcycle routes.

The Appalachian Trail in this segment passes through the solitude of densely forested ridges and along scenic gorges with cascading, pristine trout streams. It crosses alpine meadows with spectacular views resembling the big sky panoramas of the West, and climbs Virginia's three highest peaks: Mount Rogers, Whitetop Mountain and Pine Mountain. The woodlands range from Appalachian hardwoods to northern type spruce/fir stands. The open balds en route contain azalea and rhododendron gardens, cranberry bogs, and prolific blackberry and blueberry bushes.

For points south of Damascus, see the Holston Mountain chapter.

Access 1: Damascus to Feathercamp Access on US-58
Trail segment distance: 4.5 miles, one way.
Difficulty rating: Moderate, but strenuous climbs, treacherous footing when wet.
Connecting trails: Virginia Creeper, Iron Mountain, and Feathercamp.

Damascus, Virginia, is a popular resupply, mail drop, and layover point for through hikers on the Appalachian Trail. The trail passes through town one block southwest of the main street, joins the **Virginia Creeper Trail** briefly, then crosses US-58 east of town (0.3 mile before the intersection of Highway 91 south).

Wooden steps and a sign note the trail, which is located on the north side of US-58, and its white painted blazes are also visible. There is limited parking along the roadside. The Virginia Creeper Trail (an old railroad swath) continues along the south side of the highway and up Laurel Creek.

The Appalachian Trail sets out by climbing the southern foot of Iron Mountain to Cuckoo Gap, a distance of 2.5 miles. The route up the mountain is a strenuous climb, with an increase of roughly 1,000 feet in altitude, by a serpentine course.

The white blazed trail intersects the **Iron Mountain Trail**, marked with yellow painted blazes, near the gap. The routes run parallel along the summit at the 3,000 feet level, until the white trail turns eastward, leaving the mountain to return to US-58 at the Feathercamp Access. A motorcycle trail, USFS-4553, also crosses the white route, at about ¼ mile from the access. The rutted motorcycle track travels from US-58 to the top of the mountain, and intersects with other bike routes along the crest.

Access 2: Feathercamp crossing, US-58, north to Beartree Gap.
Trail segment distance: 4.6 miles, approximate, one way.
Difficulty rating: Mostly moderate, but some steep grades.
Connecting trails: Feathercamp, Virginia Creeper, and Beartree.

The Appalachian Trail distance from Damascus to the Feathercamp access is 4.5 miles. Highway 58 links the two access points, with the Feathercamp crossing at 3.4 miles east of the US-58/91 south junction, near Damascus. There is a sign, white painted blazes are visible, and there is turnout parking.

The continuing Appalachian Trail route north begins on the south side of Highway 58. The white marked path crosses a good footbridge near the access, and approaches the **Virginia Creeper** in a few hundred yards. The route is a relatively easy amble for the first couple of miles, running beside the Virginia Creeper. The Appalachian Trail turns sharply up Cross Fork Mountain (at about ½ mile before reaching the Taylors Valley Community and the Taylors Valley Access 3). The white blazes lead a tour of the higher ridges, with some steep inclines and several switchbacks. There are occasional screened views and overlooks from these ridges.

The Appalachian Trail then follows the crest of Straight Mountain high above Laurel Creek's canyon and intersects the **Beartree Gap Trail**, roughly estimated, at 4.6 miles from the Feathercamp Access. This purple/magenta blazed track leads north to US-58 in 0.3 mile (Access 4), Beartree Recreation Area in 0.5 mile, and on to the **Iron Mountain Trail** in 3 miles.

Feathercamp Trail

The Feathercamp Trail is marked with blue painted blazes and turns northeastward from the white marked route about 100 yards from the north side of US-58 and the Feathercamp Access (but traveling south on the Appalachian Trail). Although rated moderate in difficulty, this is a more primitive, single-file type footpath, and may be ill-defined, steep and overgrown in places. It travels 2.2 miles to meet the **Iron Mountain Trail** at the Sandy Flats Shelter, near USFS-90.

Route 90 turns north from Highway 58 at 2.7 miles east from the Feathercamp Access. Traveling along this single lane gravel road, the yellow blazes and the Iron Mountain Trail sign are intersected at 1.4 miles, and the blue blazes of the Feathercamp Trail at 1.9 miles from the highway.

Also, see the Iron Mountain Trail section.

Access 3: Taylor's Valley, Appalachian Trail via Virginia Creeper.

The **Virginia Creeper Trail** can be met by road in the Taylor's Valley Community, on State Route 725. This secondary road turns from Highway 91 about 2.5 miles south of 91's junction with US-58.

West on the Virginia Creeper, back toward Damascus, the Appalachian Trail blazes are noted in about ½ mile on the right side of the old railroad swath.

East on the Virginia Creeper, the route is through an area of small farms and cabins for around one mile, before returning to the wooded hollows. After another 3 miles, the Appalachian Trail is joined again for about 1 ½ miles until the crossing of VA-859 access points, noted later in the Appalachian Trail narrative.

Distance from the US-58/VA-91 junction to the VA-859 access via the Virginia Creeper is approximately 12 miles.

Access 4: Beartree Gap
Trail distances: VA-859 3 miles; US-58 at Summit Cut, 4.9 miles.
Difficulty rating: Moderate to difficult.
Connecting trail: Virginia Creeper.

Beartree Gap Trail

The Beartree Gap Trail crosses US-58 at 3.8 miles east from the Feathercamp access (6 miles from US-58/91 south at Damascus). There is a sign and possibly room to park one car beside the roadway. Additional parking is available at the Beartree Recreation Area. Driving from Damascus, you will see the Beartree Recreation Area turn on the left, ¼ mile before reaching the Beartree Gap Trail crossing of U.S. 58. There is a sign for the camping/picnic area, and the road is noted as Route 837. A large paved parking area for the trail is on the right, just after the turn.

From the parking lot, the **Beartree Gap Trail**, traveling southeast, connects with the **Appalachian Trail** in about ½ mile of easy walking. Northward the purple blazed trail is a moderately rated path of about 2.5 miles, terminating at the yellow blazed **Iron Mountain Trail**.

Paved Route 837 continues past this parking area for 4 miles to the camping area and passes several beaver ponds with wooden walkways en route. The road ends at the trail head for the **Lum Trail**.

Continuing Appalachian Trail route:
From the Beartree Gap Trail junction, the Appalachian Trail descends back into Laurel-Whitetop gorge to intersect the **Virginia Creeper Trail** and continues with it for over one mile, crossing a high trestle above Big Laurel Creek en route. The Creeper and the white blazed trail then separate to meet VA-859 at different points.

This segment is roughly 3 miles.

Access 5: Virginia 859, Appalachian and Virginia Creeper Trails.

Virginia 859 turns south from US-58 at 2.3 miles east of the Beartree Gap access. The white blazes of the Appalachian Trail may be noted on either side of the rough lane at 0.8 mile from the highway. There is no parking at the crossing, but a turnout is a short distance farther along the lane. Continuing along VA-859, the Virginia Creeper Trail crosses in 2.3 miles from US-58.

North by foot from the VA-859 crossing, the Appalachian Trail intersects US-58 again in 1.9 miles, in the Summit Cut area. Some steep inclines are encountered on Lost Mountain en route and, appropriately for the name, the segment can be difficult and overgrown.

Virginia Creeper Trail

The Virginia Creeper Trail is a popular hiker, bicycle, horse and jogger trail, as well as cross-country ski route when there is snow. The rails and cross ties have been removed, leaving an even walking surface, and trestles at the stream crossings have recently been improved with board walkways.

Beginning at Abingdon, Virginia, it is rated very easy throughout its 50 miles. From Abingdon to Damascus the right-of-way is flanked mostly by rolling farmlands. There are detours where the path crosses the Holston River and US-58 en route.

Continuing east from Damascus, the Virginia Creeper Trail runs parallel to US-58 south of the highway, along popular trout stream Laurel Creek. The trail is usually within one hundred yards of the highway for the first 3 miles after the US-58/VA-91 south junction. There are several places to park along the road shoulder. Signs note the trail, but the trestles and wide swath of the old rail bed are obvious with out them.

The wide, swift flowing stream has several tumbling sections and quiet pools used as swimming holes in summer. The Creeper turns toward the mountain recesses just before the Feathercamp Access (Access 2) of the **Appalachian Trail**. The white blazed route can be seen around the 21 mile post. The white blazed footpath is in tandem with the Creeper, frequently within 100 feet of the north side of the rail bed, tracking the bottom of the ridge, until it turns sharply uphill, in nearly 2 miles.

The **Virginia Creeper Trail** continues up Laurel-Whitetop Gorge from this divergence and reaches the isolated Taylors Valley Community (See Access 3) in about ½ mile. The route is generally eastward through the picturesque community, then passes several small farms and hunting cabins. Returning to public lands in about one mile, the route follows the meanders of the gorge into the mountains. The Virginia Creeper is an easy, direct stroll through the gorge and meets the Appalachian Trail again beyond Beartree Gap. The Appalachian Trail joins the Creeper for about 1½ miles, and the white trail also uses the high trestle of the old rail bridge to cross the gorge. Views from this high span (near the VA-859 junction) are dramatic. There have been discussions and plans to extend the Creeper beyond its current terminus, but currently the trail from here to Damascus is approximately 12 miles.

Part of the picturesque Taylor's Valley Community along the Virginia Creeper Trail.

Whitetop Mountain Area

Continuing Appalachian Trail...

Map for this area is on 197.

Access 6: Summit Cut/Highway 58.

The **Appalachian Trail** crossing of US-58 at Summit Cut is 2.5 miles east from the Virginia 603 junction. (Route 603 runs parallel to Iron Mountain to Route 16, and has several trail access points along it, noted later in the Appalachian Trail narrative and Iron Mountain Trail segment.) Although the white blazes of the Appalachian Trail are not prominent, the trail begins its assent of the Beech Mountain shoulder of Whitetop Mountain from here. Initially, the route is though private holdings but returns to the public trust after the Route 601 crossing.

Snow-covered trees on Whitetop Mountain.

A lone hiker scales Whitetop Mountain with the Buzzard Rock viewpoint in the background.

Access 7: Virginia Route 601

The Appalachian Trail meets Virginia 601 after about one mile of moderate walking. This secondary lane makes a loop from US-58; it turns from the north side of the highway at one mile, and again at 4 miles, east from the Virginia 603 junction.

From VA-601, the path up Whitetop is a steady climb of 2.3 miles to the Buzzard Rock viewpoint. This butte has excellent panoramic views of the Virginia, North Carolina and Tennessee Mountains.

From Buzzard Rock, the trail continues upward over the Whitetop meadows, and the walking becomes much easier. This open area is broken with clusters of wind and frost-dwarfed trees; their gnarled arms give dramatic scale to the endless, folding landscape.

Continuing uphill along the Appalachian Trail from Buzzard Rock, rocky USFS-89 is about ½ mile above the overview. This road, with numerous parking and turnout areas, makes a loop around the south face of the mountain, just below the peak with its evergreen forest and FAA installation. The foot trail follows this lane for about ¼ mile before returning to the forest.

Access 8: Whitetop Mountain on USFS-89.

Route 89 turns northwest from VA-600 at 1.7 miles north of the VA-600/US-58 junction. (VA-600 also connects with VA-603 in the next valley to the north, with the Elk Garden Access passed en route.)

Atop the mountain the Appalachian Trail blazes are noticeable along the lane in the bald area.

At a point approximately 2 miles, by USFS-89 from VA-600 the white-blazed footpath turns into the woods and slopes of Whitetop Mountain for the descent to the Elk Garden Access (this is north on the trail). This segment of 2.5 miles has a relatively easy grade. The path is mostly through mixed hardwoods until its junction with paved VA-600.

In mid to late April and early May, this trail segment presents some of the most dramatic displays of fringed phacelia mixed with yellow and red trillium, trout lilies and other wildflowers to be found anywhere. The pungent "Ramp," a wild leek considered either a delicacy or an abomination according to your taste, is also prolific along the ridge.

Mount Rogers Area

Access 9: Elk Garden on Virginia Route 600.

The Elk Garden Access, with off-road parking, is 3 miles north of the VA-600/US-58 junction, or 5.8 miles south of the VA-600/VA-603 intersection.

Excellent views that include the evergreen crown of Mount Rogers (lying slightly north of due east) are offered from the grassy pinnacles at Elk Garden.

A large, color-coded, wooden map of trails in this area stands on the east side of the fence and gate from the parking.

This access serves as trail head for routes including:

The Appalachian Trail, Virginia Highlands Horse Trail, Helton Creek/Sugar Maple Loop Trails.

Virginia Highlands Horse Trail

Marked with orange painted blazes, this old road bed takes a route nearly parallel to the **Appalachian Trail** and intersects it at least three times between Elk Garden and the northeastern boundary of Grayson Highlands State Park. It can be linked with the white marked path to make comfortable day hikes around the "Rooftop of Virginia." Note the junctions at Deep Gap and in the Grayson Highlands area for these circuits. Most of the Virginia Highlands Horse Trail is wide and easy walking; it is used as much by those on foot (or on cross-country skis in winter) as by those on horseback.

Open to hikers throughout its 48 miles, there are additional access points on VA-603, VA-16, and from Grayson Highlands State Park.

Taking the horse trail northeast from the Elk Garden gate, the first ½ mile is through open pastureland. Before leaving the meadows, the purple blazes of the **Helton Creek Loop Trail** lead downhill toward the hollows. The Helton Loop is actually a double circle route of about 5 miles of old roads and creek beds, connecting with the **Sugar Maple Loop Trail** and could present difficult going in wet weather. After turning back up the mountain, the purple trail completes its loop by rejoining the Virginia Highlands Horse Trail about a mile farther along the orange marked route.

Continuing beyond the first intersection with the Helton Creek Loop, the

The Virginia Highlands Horse Trail crosses this meadow on the high slopes of Mount Rogers, above Deep Gap.

orange blazed Horse Trail enters the woods through another gate. The second junction with the purple Loop Trail is encountered at about 1½ miles from Elk Garden, and this fork in the trail may be slightly confusing. The right branch may appear to be the main trail, but the Virginia Highlands Horse Trail is the left, uphill fork. It is another ½ mile to the converging paths at Deep Gap.

This popular camp spot is the site of an Appalachian Trail Shelter. The blue blazed **Mount Rogers Trail** (see Mount Rogers Trail entry for more details), connecting with the Grindstone Campground on VA-603, also approaches this gap about 100 yards north along the white trail. Continuing along the horse trail, it is about 3 miles to the next junction of the Appalachian Trail, approaching the northeastern boundary of Grayson Highlands State Park. This segment alternates between forest and open meadows. In these open fields, it is easy to explore along their upper edges and find the white blazed route.

From the Grayson Highlands area, the horse trail continues for several miles passing the Scales area en route to VA-603 and points northeast.

Continuing Appalachian Trail:

Maps for this area are on pages 197 and 198.

The Appalachian Trail, north from Elk Garden, leads about ⅓ mile over the meadows and pinnacle, then enters the heavily forested incline of Mount Rogers. The climb is a moderate grade with switchbacks. The single file footpath is well-maintained and clearly marked. The Deep Gap Shelter and junctions with the **Mount Rogers Trail** and **Virginia Highlands Horse Trail** are about 2 miles from Elk Garden.

The orange marked horse trail is in front of the shelter, and the blue blazes of the Mount Rogers Trail are intersected, just north of the shelter, along the white route. The Appalachian Trail skirts the southern face of the mountain, with moderate grades, for about 2 miles of densely-wooded walking, then intersects the blue blazed **Summit Spur Trail**.

Summit Spur Trail

The Summit Spur Trail is a one half mile rocky path to the peak of Mount Rogers. Rated moderate to easy, the route is through dense evergreen spruce/fir growth. This is the highest point in Virginia (5,729 feet). The path ends at the summit. There are no views.

Continuing Appalachian Trail route:

Returning to the Appalachian Trail from the summit detour, the route is over easier, rolling terrain through the open balds and berry thickets near Rhododendron Gap, reached in about 1.5 miles from the Spur. Rhododendron Gap is a major intersection of area trails. The **Pine Mountain Trail** and **Rhododendron Trail**, both with blue painted blazes, meet the Appalachian

Route of the Appalachian Trail is marked on rocks in the Rhododendron Gap area; Mount Rogers is in the background.

Trail in this area. There are wooden signs, with destinations and distances, for the converging routes. The 6,000 acre crest area is restricted to foot and horse travel only.

The meadows along the crest present dazzling views (especially during early summer when the azalea and rhododendron are in bloom) and tasty snacks in late summer (as the blueberries and blackberries ripen).

Pine Mountain Trail

The Pine Mountain Trail was once the route of the Appalachian Trail. Well marked with blue painted blazes, it has no road access. It follows the scenic

Along the Rhododendron Gap Trail between Grayson Highlands and Mount Rogers.

crest of Virginia's third highest peak northeastward to rejoin the Appalachian Trail in about 2.5 miles of easy walking. The new route of the Appalachian Trail is about 7 miles over varied terrain to their northern junction. There are signs at both ends of the trail.

Rhododendron Trail

The blue blazed Rhododendron Trail takes a more direct (and, to me more scenic) route over the pinnacles and open meadows between Rhododendron Gap and the edge of Grayson Highlands State Park than the Appalachian Trail. This route can be used as an alternate to the white-marked path, or joined with it as part of a circuit starting and returning to the state park access at Massie Gap. See a separate entry in the Grayson Highlands section for more details.

Continuing Appalachian Trail route:

From Rhododendron Gap, the north-traveling Appalachian Trail turns southward, with easy walking along the perimeter of high meadows, toward Grayson Highlands State Park. Looking downhill from these meadows, the **Virginia Highlands Horse Trail** is visible lower on the ridge. The orange blazes of the horse trail are crossed at the fence stile at the State Park boundary; the Rhododendron Trail's blue blazes intersect the white trail at the fence crossing.

Across the fence, the Appalachian Trail leads along Wilbur Ridge (used by the parks herd of wild ponies and as summer cattle pasture) and the edge of Sullivan Swamp (boggy area to north of trail). The blue marked path, descending the ridge to the Massie Gap parking/access, is met in about ½ mile.

Access 10: Massie Gap, Grayson Highlands State Park.

The Grayson Highlands State Park entrance is on US-58, about 5 miles west of the VA-16 junction. Massie Gap is approximately 5 miles by paved road from the entrance. At the gap there are a large parking area and detailed, color-coded maps of the marked trail systems. The park offers an excellent system of trails of varied length and full campground facilities in summer, when there is also a parking fee. The blue marked trail is a short connector of about ¼ mile to the top of Wilbur Ridge and intersection with the Appalachian Trail.

Another route is possible for the more adventurous. Take the **Wilson Creek Trail** from the park campground and follow the stream northward; then by unmarked, primitive trails, climb to the crest and the Appalachian Trail, near the eastern end of the summit area and park boundary—but take a good map and compass.

See Grayson Highlands Section.

Continuing Appalachian Trail route:

Continuing north on the Appalachian Trail along Wilbur Ridge from the blue trail's turn to Massie Gap, the first ½ mile is an easy stroll along the crest. There are rocky pinnacles in the open meadow area with excellent views. Then the route is steeply uphill and down dale, by moderate to strenuous trail, all the way to the VA-603 access. On leaving the park boundary, the path crosses Quebec Branch and Wilson Creek; crosses Stone Mountain to Scales, site of old cattle weighing station; then over Pine Mountain to the Old Orchard Shelter, passing the **Pine Mountain Trail** junction en route.

From the Old Orchard Shelter, it is 1.7 miles by the white path to VA-603 at Fox Creek. A primitive, unmarked, secondary path leads westward from the shelter to the **Lewis Fork Trail**.

Wild ponies graze along the northeastern end of Wilburn Ridge in the Grayson Highlands area.

Lewis Fork Trail

The Lewis Fork Trail has grey diamond blazes and, for the most part, is fairly easy to moderate in difficulty. The path may be noted on the southeast side of VA-603, about midway between the Mount Rogers and Appalachian Trail access points. This trail is another old logging road grade, so most of the slopes are gentle; it leads into the Lewis Fork Wilderness Area. There are unmarked paths connecting it to both the Appalachian Trail (at the Old Orchard Shelter) and the Mount Rogers Trail, but it dead ends at the head of Lewis Fork Creek in roughly 3.5 miles.

Rhododendron Gap area in the Mount Rogers National Recreation Area, reached by the Appalachian, Pine Mountain, Rhododendron or Virginia Highlands Horse Trail.

Additional Access Points: From VA-603, VA-16, and VA-650/USFS-84 Trail Crossings.

The Appalachian Trail crossing of VA-603 at Fox Creek has off-road parking and is noted with a sign. Route 603 runs between VA-16 at Troutdale and US-58 near Konnarock.

From the parking, the white blazed route continues north to scale Iron Mountain again and intersect its yellow marked trail on the crest in 2.2 miles. The Hurricane Campground is 4.1 miles. A secondary path leads from the Appalachian Trail to the campground/access, near the VA-650/USFS-84 junction. A sign on Highway 16 directs to the campground.

North from the Hurricane Campground diversion, the trail continues along the slope of Iron Mountain to Comers Creek Falls, which are reached in about one mile. These falls are not spectacular, probably in the 25-30 feet range, but a pleasant pause in the hardwood forest. The trail crosses VA-650 near its intersection with VA-16 in another mile.

The VA-650/VA-16 access, at Dickey Gap, is marked with a sign to the Hurricane Campground, and there is limited parking beside VA-16. The VA-650 turn is 15.2 miles from Interstate 81 at Marion.

From Dickey Gap, the Appalachian Trail reaches the Raccoon Branch Shelter in 1.6 miles. There is a side trail to High Point (for views of Rye Valley), and the blue marked **Raccoon Branch Trail** leads to the Raccoon Branch Campground on VA-16.

Distances from Dickey Gap: Trimpi Shelter, 4.2 miles; VA- 672, 5.6 miles; Holston River and VA-670, 7.7 miles; and VA-16, (as well as the terminus of this segment of the Appalachian Trail) at the Mount Rogers National Recreation Area Headquarters, estimated at 16 miles.

Grayson Highlands State Park Trails

Grayson Highlands State Park offers eight hiking trails, ranging from short and easy to moderate in both length and difficulty. The **Rhododendron Trail** begins at Massie Gap and connects with the **Appalachian Trail** on Wilburn Ridge. The **Wilson Creek Trail**, via primtive routes, also meets the Maine to Georgia footpath on the northeast end of the ridge. The panoramic views from the park trails are some of the best in the region. Other attractions include Cabin Creek Falls, a wild pony herd, restored mountain homestead, and connections to trails in the adjoining Mount Rogers National Recreation Area.

How to Get There

Map for this area is on page 198.

Grayson Highlands State Park is located in southwest Virginia's Grayson County, near Mouth of Wilson. The park entrance is on US-58. From Interstate 81 it can be approached from Abingdon, via Damascus, passing numerous trails in the Mount Rogers National Recreation area en route, or from Marion along VA-16, then west on US-58. Secondary routes from Chilhowie and by Mount Rogers area trails are noted in listings for the **Virginia Highlands Horse Trail, Rhododendron Trail, Appalachian Trail** and others.

Approximate mileages from the park entrance are: Marion, 35 miles; Galax 45; Abingdon, 40.

From US-58 a spur road leads 5 miles to the park gate, where a parking fee is charged in summer.

Beyond the contact station, the road continues up the mountain with turns to the campground and picnic area. There is a large parking area at Massie Gap, and several hiker and horse routes begin or end here.

There are plaques at Massie Gap noting the heads of converging trails, and a large wooden map across the meadow shows their routes.

Continuing past Massie Gap, the road continues to another parking area atop the mountain, with other trail connections and view points nearby.

Appalachian Trail along Wilburn Ridge near its junction with the Rhododendron Trail in the Grayson Highlands area.

Rhododendron Trail

also called Wilburn Ridge Trail
    Trail distance: 2.5 miles, one way.
    Difficulty rating: Mostly easy.
    Connecting routes: Appalachian Trail, Pine Mountain Trail and
Virginia Highlands Horse Trail.

This trail offers exceptional panoramic views of the rugged alpine scenery for which the Grayson Highlands and Mount Rogers areas are renowned. The route connects with other trails for circuit walks of varied length.

The trail head is at Massie Gap, marked by a plaque. The route is marked with blue painted blazes on rocks and trees.

From the parking area northward, it is a short graded climb of ¼ mile to the top of Wilburn Ridge. Here the white blazes of the Appalachian Trail are met. Both routes follow the crest, along with numerous cow and pony paths.

Cattle and a small herd of wild ponies graze on the high meadows. The size of the pony herd is kept in check by a fall roundup and auction to benefit the local fire department. These animals (as well as deer and other wildlife) help keep the highlands cleared of brush and trees, contributing to the magnificent vistas. The ponies are accustomed to people traveling along the trail, and can be photographed or watched, but should not be approached, stalked, or interfered with.

From the **Appalachian Trail** junction on the Wilburn Ridge summit, high buttes can be seen on either end of the crest. There are commanding 360 degree views from these high points. The easiest to reach is along the white blazed trail eastward (northbound) for about ½ mile.

Sullivan Swamp lies to the north, a boggy area in the swag toward the park boundary. The blue blazes skirt this area before reaching a fence stile (about ¾ mile from the parking). Across the stile are the orange blazes of the **Virginia Highlands Horse Trail**, and Mount Rogers National Recreation Area is entered. The Rhododendron Trail continues to the north and northwest from this junction. Meadows, small stands of spruce/fir, and rocky pinnacles are crossed as you follow the blue blazes.

Looking ahead at the blue trail markers, they appear to be painted on sheer cliffs, but the route has been chosen carefully so that the climb is rarely more difficult than walking up a steep flight of stairs. You have to watch your step, of course, but the views are awesome.

Catawba Rhododendron bloom sometime between mid-June to early July, depending on the severity of the winter and spring weather. Like the more prolific gardens of Roan Mountain, deep pink blossoms render the highlands almost iridescent during their peak and give Rhododendron Gap its name. There are large beds of flame azalea as well.

Shortly after descending these high meadows and buttes, the blue blazed route rejoins the **Appalachian Trail** near Rhododendron Gap. There is a sign at the gap pointing to the continuing route to Mount Rogers, and a short distance along the path another sign notes the turn of the blue blazed **Pine Mountain Trail**.

The Rhododendron Gap Trail, as described here, may also be listed as the Wilburn Ridge Trail, but whichever name is used, the route travels by blue blazes from Massie Gap and crosses Wilburn Ridge to connect with other paths at Rhododendron Gap.

Map for this area is on page 198.

Cabin Creek Trail
1.9 mile loop—Easy

This is an enjoyable easy walk to a series of small waterfalls on Cabin Creek.

Starting point of the walk is at Massie Gap. From the parking, at the sign noting the trail, the route bears left; then it crosses a small jeep or horse road and enters the woods through an arching laurel tunnel. After reaching a small brook, the Cabin Creek Trail divides to make a loop past the falls. The left track follows a small stream, and is the steeper of the two. Stone slab bridges span the spring branch on the slope.

The loop totals only 1.9 miles. In addition to the falls, the trail also has a stand of Big Tooth Aspens, rare this far south, which turn bright golden yellow in fall to resemble the quaking Aspens of the west. The stream supports native Brook Trout and Rainbow Trout (fishing is allowed by permit), and the trail is lined with blueberry bushes.

Wilson Creek Trail

The Wilson Creek and Stampers Branch Trails can be linked to cross most of the eastern side of the park. The Wilson Creek Trail begins from the concession area at the campground. There are signs to the campground from the main park road.

The trail head is marked, and the route leads downhill from the camping area to the creek. It is wide and clearly defined.

Primitive trails lead along the stream in both directions. Upstream, it is

Cabin Creek Falls in the Grayson Highlands State Park.

possible to join the **Appalachian Trail** in 2 to 3 miles of unmarked paths along the cascading stream, then up the northeast slope of Wilburn Ridge. For the more adventurous, unofficial paths also lead downstream toward the picnic area and the homestead cabin; these old timber roads travel along the creek and can be difficult going. Allow plenty of time and take a map and compass.

Stampers Branch Trail
Moderate—2 miles, one way.

A more challenging course, the Stampers Branch Trail has steep climbs. It connects the campground with trails and facilities atop Haw Orchard Mountain. The trail is rated moderate, with an altitude change of 600 feet in two miles.

The route is clear and well traveled, with signs at its ends. From the campground, the course crosses two small streams, climbs the ridge, and crosses the main park road. From here the trail is steeply uphill to the top of the mountain, where the **Twin Pinnacles, Big Pinnacles** and **Listening Rock Trails** can be explored in the summit area.

Twin Pinnacles and Big Pinnacles Trails
2 mile loop—Easy.

The Twin Pinnacles and Big Pinnacles Trails link to make a loop around the pinnacles atop the mountain. Starting from the parking/visitors center and end of the main park road, the routes are well marked and within the easy range. The path around the peaks to the northwest offers spectacular 360 degree vistas, and is in the 2 mile range for the round trip. The top of the mountain may be closed to vehicles in winter, but trails from Massie Gap and the Stampers Branch Trail can be climbed to the summit. The unmarked path from Massie Gap leads about ½ mile southward up the mountain from near the rest rooms.

Listening Rock/Wildcat Trail
1.5 miles, loop—Easy.

The Listening Rock Trail/Wildcat Trail also makes a loop from the Visitors Center atop Haw Orchard Mountain. Traveling south, then west from the parking area, the trail is approximately 1.5 miles round trip and is rated moderate. Spectacular views are offered from rocky overlooks. After reaching the overlook, at the southern point of the trail, the route turns toward the Buzzard Rock Overlook, just off the main park road near the Visitors Center.

The trail up Wilburn Ridge from Massie Gap in the Grayson Highlands State Park.

Rock Horse Ridge Trail

This trail starts at the picnic site parking. The approximately 2 mile trip offers views of the farmlands east of the park. For explorers it is possible to connect with the lower Wilson Creek Trail. The path is in the easy to moderate range.

More Mount Rogers National Recreation Area Trails

Mount Rogers Trail
From VA-603 to Appalachian Trail at Deep Gap
Trail distances: Appalachian Trail, 4 miles; Mount Rogers peak, 6.5 miles, one way estimates.
Difficulty rating: Mostly moderate.
Connecting trails: Appalachian Trail and Virginia Highlands Horse Trail.

The Mount Rogers Trail climbs the north slope of the mountain of the same name. The footpath is well maintained and marked with blue painted blazes. It is a popular woodland trek, with several opportunities for circuit walks within the Mount Rogers system of National Recreation Trails.

How to Get There

Maps for this area are on pages 197 and 198.

There are three main road approaches from Interstate 81 to the trail head near Grindstone Campground:

1. From Abingdon, Virginia, take US-58 east; pass through Damascus and turn onto VA-603 near Konnarock. Grindstone Campground is roughly 8 miles from the junction, with VA-600 crossed en route. The trail can be joined from the campground or at 0.5 mile farther on VA-603, where there is a sign and parking.

2. From Chilhowie, Virginia, turn onto VA-762 at the Highway 107 exit, then onto VA-600, after 4 miles; then turn left onto VA-603 in another 8.6 miles. The Grindstone Campground is about 4.5 miles from the VA-600/603 junction.

3. From Marion, Virginia, take Route 16 east and turn right onto VA-603 before reaching Troutdale. Parking and trail head signs are just over 5 miles from the VA-16/603 junction.

The Mount Rogers Trail can be reached at its terminus at Deep Gap by the connecting **Appalachian Trail** and **Virginia Highlands Horse Trail**. They both travel from either the Elk Garden or Massie Gap access points to Deep Gap. See the Appalachian Trail section.

The Trail

The Mount Rogers Trail begins from the off-road parking site beside VA-603, where blue markings and a sign are clearly visible. The mountain pinnacle is about 6.5 miles away by foot. The trail can also be accessed by a spur from the Grindstone Campground, which adds about ½ mile to the walk.

The path is through mature hardwood forest, and there are no views until you reach connecting routes beyond Deep Gap. As with most area National Recreation Trails, the walkway is clearly marked and well tended. There are footbridges over the few trickles of water along the ridge. Signs at strategic points direct hikers to connecting routes, and note mileage to major landmarks.

Initially, the trail heads westerly, gradually rising along the ridge for nearly ½ mile, then switches back the opposite direction for another ½ mile, zig-zagging its way to the top of the first ridge. On the plateau, a sign indicates the direction of the **Lewis Fork Trail** along a primitive, unmarked path to the left. The Mount Rogers Trail continues straight, toward the south. The remaining slopes are gradual, until the summit and the **Appalachian Trail** is joined about 100 yards northeast of the Deep Gap Shelter. The popular camping area in the flat of the gap is about four miles from VA-603 and is the terminus of the blue blazed path.

The **Virginia Highlands Horse Trail** passes directly in front of the Deep Gap Shelter. Elk Garden on VA-600 is a couple of miles west by either the horse track or white blazed footpath. East on either of the parallel routes requires moderate climbing up the mountain shoulder to meadows with excellent views and then goes on to the Grayson Highlands. However, to reach the evergreen capped peak of Virginia's highest mountain (at 5,729 feet), the **Appalachian Trail** must be followed for approximately two miles to the **Summit Spur Trail**. This is a moderately graded ½ mile diversion from the white blazed path, and it is marked with a sign. There are no views from the peak, but the evergreen forest crowning the crest is similar to forest 800 miles north in Canada.

Grassy Branch Trail
3 miles, estimated, one way—moderate/easy.

The Grassy Branch Trail leads along a wide, abandoned rail grade. Rated easy to moderate, with weed growth in late summer, it is also a popular cross-country ski trail in winter. There is a sign for the trail on VA-603, between the VA-600/603 junction and Grindstone Campground. The blue blazed trail has shallow stream crossings, and becomes steeper on the VA-600 end, reaching the roadway between Elk Garden and the above VA-600/603 junction.

Iron Mountain Trail

North From Damascus, Virginia
Trail segment distance: 11 miles, one way estimate.
Difficulty rating: Moderate.

Maps of the area show the Iron Mountain Trail ascending from near the 91 North/US-58 division at Damascus. As far as I can tell, it heads up Fourth Street, a narrow lane resembling a driveway; I recommend instead, that you rejoin the **Appalachian Trail** to climb this slope of the mountain. Atop the crest at Cuckoo Gap, the yellow blazes of the Iron Mountain Trail can be found.

East from Damascus on US-58, just before the Route 91 turn south, the Appalachian Trail has steps leading up the ridge into the woods. White blazes and a sign mark the trail crossing.

The white blazed route takes a serpentine course up the mountain (a 1,000 foot climb) to reach Cuckoo Gap in 2.5 miles. In the summit area, short connector paths lead to the yellow blazes of the Iron Mountain Trail, and motorcycle routes are also encountered in the vicinity.

The courses trace the same ridge lines along the summit for a mile or so, then the yellow trail turns more northerly and continues in the crest area, while the white trail edges down the south side of the ridge to return to US-58 at the Feathercamp Access. A wide motorcycle track also crosses the summit, traveling from US-58 to connect with the Foothills Trail on the northern, lower contour of the mountain.

The yellow painted blazes continue along the undulating terrain of the ridge tops toward the Sandy Flats Shelter and the intersection of the blue blazed

Feathercamp Trail (see the Feathercamp and Appalachian Trail entries). U.S. Forest Service Route 90 is about ¼ mile beyond these points.

Attention has been given to providing separate walking and motorcycle routes where practical. Two Iron Mountain routes may be encountered, as from Route 90, but there are notices for bike or foot travel.

Road Access from US-58/USFS-90 and USFS-837

Driving east on US-58 from the Highway 91 south junction, you will encounter motorcycle route 4553, at 2.9 miles (it crosses the mountain in Cuckoo Gap area in about 1.5 miles); Feathercamp Access to Appalachian and Feathercamp Trails, at 3.2 miles; USFS-90, at 5.9 miles (turn left and drive 1.4 miles to the trail head); USFS-837, turning toward Beartree Campground, at 6.7 miles. Driving along USFS-837, the Beartree Trail crosses at 0.3 mile, connecting to the Iron Mountain Trail in about 3 miles; turn at the end of the road 4 miles from Highway 58, the **Lum Trail** departs from beside the rest rooms to join the Iron Mountain Trail at Shaw Gap near the Straight Branch Shelter in one mile. From the shelter, the VA-600 access is another mile by the yellow blazed route.

Iron Mountain Trail

North From Sandy Flats Area, USFS-90, to VA Highway-600.
Trail segment distance: 6 miles, one way estimate.
Difficulty rating: Moderate.

From the Sandy Flats Shelter at the USFS-90 junction, there are several options for circuit hikes or diversions from the Iron Mountain Trail. Highway 58 is 1.4 miles downhill to the south. North on USFS-90, the intersection of Route 615 (an off-road vehicle track) departs toward VA-604 and points north and east, in ½ mile. The Iron Mountain Motorcycle Trail, turning toward the southwest, is noted with a sign just up the hill in another 0.1 mile. Route 90 terminates at the ridge high point where the Feathercamp Fire Tower once stood. This knob is rapidly growing up in small timber which blocks the views, and all that remains of the tower are steps where the base stood. From this knob, trails descend both east and west, but have apparently been abandoned. The sign for the path west has been removed and the blazes painted over with black. The track east is more defined, since it was once used by vehicles. Returning to the Iron Mountain Trail: From the Route 90 junction, the

A maple tree on the Iron Mountain Trail near Skull Gap.

route northeast is moderate to easy walking, with the path well defined and marked with yellow painted blazes on trees. The **Beartree Gap Trail** is crossed at about 2 miles; the Straight Branch Shelter and intersection of the **Lum Trail** from the Beartree Campground is at 4.8 miles; and VA-600 at about 5.8 miles.

Road Access from VA-600 at Skull Gap:

Continuing east on US-58 from the USFS-837 junction the access points are: Beartree Gap Trail, 0.3 miles; Straight Mountain Trail, 0.6 miles; Route 859 (for the Appalachian and Virginia Creeper Trails connections), 2.6 miles; and VA-603/ US-58 junction, at 3 miles. Route 603 crosses VA-600 en route to Grindstone Campground and VA-16 at Troutdale. At the VA-600/603 intersection turn left, toward Chilhowie, and the Skull Gap Access is 2.8 miles, at the crest of the mountain. There is plenty of parking and yellow blazes are visible along the road.

Access from Chilhowie/Interstate 81:

The VA-600 Skull Gap access can be approached from the Chilhowie area. From Interstate 81 take the Route 107 exit, turn onto VA-762 traveling east, and 4 miles turn onto VA-600, beginning the climb of the mountain. The Iron Mountain Trail head south is 10 miles from I-81, and the leg north is just ahead on the left, beyond the USFS-84 junction.

From Skull Gap, Route 84 is a rough forest track running parallel to the Iron Mountain Trail. It is not suitable for cars with low ground clearance, and may require four wheel drive during bad weather. Route 828, connecting USFS-84 to VA-603 near the Grindstone Campground, turns right at about 4 miles. Route 828 crosses the Iron Mountain Trail near the Cherry Tree shelter. Continuing on Route 84 the Hurricane Campground (at the junction of 84/650) is another 4 miles.

Additional Access points on VA-603:

From the VA-600/603 junction, drive east toward Troutdale. The **Grassy Ridge Trail** head is on the right in 2 miles; Route 828, which crosses the **Iron Mountain Trail** near the Cherry Tree Shelter, turns northward in 4.3 miles; and Grindstone Campground is just ahead, on the south side of the road. The blue blazed **Mount Rogers Trail** is 4.9 miles; **Lewis Fork Trail**, at 5.7 miles; a horse trail, at 5.9 miles; the **Appalachian Trail**, at 6.6 miles; and VA-16 is 10.8 miles from the VA-600 junction.

The **Appalachian Trail**, traveling north from VA-603, crosses the **Iron Mountain Trail** in 2.2 miles. Route 741, which turns north from VA-603 just east of the Appalachian Trail parking, also meets the **Iron Mountain Trail**, 0.2 mile before its junction of VA-16.

Wild grape vines in the Comers Creek area.

Access points from Marion, Virginia, along Highway 16:

From Interstate 81, turn south onto VA-16, toward Troutdale. The Mount Rogers National Recreation Area Headquarters and the crossing of the **Appalachian Trail** are 6 miles; the **Virginia Highlands Horse Trail** is at 12 miles. The **Appalachian Trail** can also be met at the VA-650 turn to the Hurricane Campground, 15.2 miles from I-81. The **Appalachian Trail** can be followed to the campground in 2.3 miles, and on to the **Iron Mountain Trail** intersection in 4 miles.

Continuing on VA-16 to a point 15.7 miles from I-81, the **Iron Mountain Trail** crosses Highway 16 just before the VA-741 turn. Yellow blazes for the trail head south lead uphill toward the west. The trail head north is directly across the highway from the VA-16/741 junction, between two white posts.

Iron Mountain Trail

Northeast from Skull Gap, VA-600/USFS-84 to Highway 16:
Trail segment distance: 10 miles, estimated, one way.
Difficulty rating: Moderate.

From VA-600 the Iron Mountain Trail crosses the paved road near the Skull Gap picnic area and USFS-84 junction. The trail runs a short distance along the paved roadway, with yellow painted blazes visible on trees. There is no room to park where the southwestern link of the trail emerges from the wood, but there is plenty at the northeast trail head and at the route 84 junction.

The trail from Skull Gap to the Troutdale area runs almost due east, along a wide, well maintained swath. There are climbs, but most of the grades are gradual.

In fall and spring the area has colors that, due to the varied flora, are nearly psychedelic. Early spring probably displays the numbers of species better than does the intense hues of fall, since the budding leaves are of differing colors and shades, and many (such as the tulip poplar, service berry and cucumber tree) also have showy flowers.

The stroll along the summit is pleasant, with occasional dips through the gaps. A portion of the route leads along a closed forest road, passing the Round Top and Double Top areas before reaching the Cherry Tree Shelter after approximately 4 miles. Route 828 is about ½ mile beyond the shelter; turning left onto the road leads back to USFS-84, while right leads downhill to the Grindstone Campground.

Continuing on the **Iron Mountain Trail**, the **Appalachian Trail** is met in just under 2 miles. The two trails run nearly parallel again, with the yellow blazes along the summit and the white path taking a longer route, 1,000 feet down the slope. The Iron Mountain Trail reaches Route 741 near its intersection with VA-16 in about 3 more miles, while the Appalachian Trail reaches the Hurricane Campground on Route 650 in just over 4 miles.

A scenic treat near this end of the trail is Comers Creek Falls. They are far from dramatic, but are along a pleasant tumbling creek. The head of the creek is passed near the Iron Mountain Trail's junction with Route 741 and secondary paths meander with the stream. The cascades, reached by the Appalachian Trail, are about one mile from either the campground or Route 650 near its turn from VA-16 at Dickey Gap.

This is the northeastern limit of the area covered by this guidebook, but area maps show the Iron Mountain Trail continuing along the mountain's backbone.

More Tennessee Trails

Bays Mountain Park Trails

Bays Mountain Park, which is owned and maintained by the City of Kingsport, Tennessee, has several hiking trails. Most are within the difficulty range of easy and lead along old roadways or well defined and developed walkways.

The **Lakeside Trail** is the most popular path. It is well traveled, beginning as a paved walk near the visitor center and circling the old city reservoir. Varied lakeside flora and wildlife within the preserve is viewed along the path's 2.3 miles.

A longer walk follows old lanes around the park perimeter, passing several radio and relay installations and a fire tower en route. Estimated at 11.5 miles in length, there are views at several points.

Less defined and more challenging footpaths include: **Bays Ridge Trail**, 2.6 miles; **Pretty Ridge Trail**, 2.3 miles; and the **Indian Pipes Trail**, 2.5 miles. There is a large engraved wooden map near the park headquarters building, and maps are available at the visitors center.

The park offers a nature interpretive center, planetarium, zoo and related programs throughout the year, but use of the area is restricted to park schedules, generally the daylight hours. There is an entrance fee.

The park is reached by following signs from the TN-93/Interstate-181 junction.

Buffalo Mountain Trails

Buffalo Mountain Park near Johnson City, Tennessee, offers several hiker trails of varied length and difficulty. The developed paths are reached from the southeast side of town, by way of the road up the foot of the mountain toward the radio and TV towers. There are small yellow and brown signs on South Roan Street, Buffalo Street and Cherokee Road directing to the park. The main trail head is at the picnic area, where there is a sign. About 100 yards along this path, at the first trail junction, there is another sign noting the various foot trails and their distances. Printed, self directing maps are also available at this point.

Viewing the Johnson City area from the White Rocks Trail on Buffalo Mountain.

All of the paths are well maintained, color-coded with painted blazes, and signs mark the trail intersections. There are excellent views of the city from Huckleberry Knob and from White Rocks bluff. Mountain laurel, flame azalea, lady slippers and trillium are prolific in May and June. The forest is mostly a mixture of regrowth pine and native hardwoods.

All seven paths within the park preserve can easily be walked in a day. Most of the routes are easy, but some strenuous climbing is required along the White Rock, High Ridge and Stairstep Ridge walks. Hours are posted at the gate, but parking is also provided outside the barrier for hiker access.

From the entrance gate, along the paved road (in the first sharp bend) another gate bars unauthorized vehicles from the steep tower road, however, it can be walked to intersect the White Rock Trail on the southeast edge of the park. The gravel road to the towers is also used as a horse trail.

Trail 1 and paths on the western side of the park are reached by a new paved loop road through the picnic area, or by an old trail from the gate.

Atop the mountain, the footpaths circle the knob and transmitter towers. An old horse trail that travels for several miles along the summit turns south from the path connecting White Rocks (Trail 7) and the High Ridge Trail (Trail 4), at about ¼ mile from the gravel road and the towers, near the western park boundary.

The **Buffalo Mountain Horse Trail** is wide and clear. There are occasional yellow metal diamond markers, but there are also opportunities to take wrong branches of the lane. It travels generally to the southwest to terminate on the Pinnacle Mountain Fire Tower Road.

The old Buffalo Mountain Trail leads mostly along the mountain's spine. It can also be reached from the Cherokee Road area. Two access points are:

1. Drive south on Cherokee Road, TN-67; turn onto Lone Oak Road, across from Cherokee School, and at 2.7 miles a small creek is crossed. The trail beside it can be followed to the crest of the mountain.

The path from the pavement is moderately graded and climbs along the creek. In less than ½ mile, an old road is joined for the remaining distance to the summit gap. Distance is about 1 mile.

Turning northeast from the gap, proceed along the crest on a horse/hiker path with occasional yellow diamond markers. Estimated distance to the communications sites and other developed trails at the north shoulder of the mountain is 3.5 miles.

Southwest from the gap, the trail leads toward the Pinnacle Mountain fire tower. This link is more demanding and is in the 4 mile range.

2. Continuing along Lone Oak Road past the point mentioned above, there are several trail bike routes and closed forest roads turning up the mountain. At 5.5 miles from Cherokee Road, USFS-188 turns toward the crest. If the gate is open, the gravel road can be driven to near the fire tower and the trail head.

Clark's Creek/Buckeye Falls Trail
Distance: 3-4 miles, one way estimated—Difficult.

This is a creek side walk to a high waterfall, and all that's needed to make it dramatic is more water.

Road access: Go 5 miles west on TN-107, from the TN-81/107 junction between Jonesborough and Erwin, then turn south onto the paved road beside Clark's Creek, across from the Enon Church. The National Forest boundary

A hunter explores the bluff below Buckeye Falls in the Clark's Creek area.

is passed in 1.5 miles. This road can be driven for another 2-3 miles, depending on your vehicle and depth of water at several fords.

The Trail

The trail head is at the end of USFS-25 at some earth mound barriers. Yellow painted blazes mark the footpath, which is an old road following the stream. The stream is several yards wide, and there are several creek crossings.

There is a turn at about ¼ mile from the barriers which is easy to miss. A giant hollow tree lies beside the creek near this branch of the stream. The wider stream and path continue straight, but the trail to the falls crosses the ravine to take the lesser route. This path runs generally southwest, and it still has intermittent yellow blazes.

The path along the tumbling branch is lined with a variety of hardwoods, but more noticeable are the paper bark birch trees and large groves of buckeyes and hemlocks. After about 2 miles, a smaller stream branches left. Take the next branch of the stream left, about ¼ mile farther on. This fork has an arrow pointing to it, and a large "B" is carved into the bark of a tree in the junction. This unlikely-looking spring branch runs east and southeast and has some yellow blazes.

The grade gets steep as the stream and path merge. Buckeye Falls are about

1 ½ mile from the fork. In winter the sheer cliffs are coated with ice for 300 feet or more from the minor branch. In dry weather there are no falls.

Trail of the Lonesome Pine

The Trail of the Lonesome Pine began as an ambitious project during the mid-1970's. As proposed, it would have traveled the length of Clinch Mountain from near Roanoke, Virginia, to near Knoxville, Tennessee. There it would have connected with the Cumberland Trail and continued south to Chattanooga. Sadly, neither trail has been completed as initially planned, although efforts continue.

The Lonesome Pine route in the Tennessee link ran into difficulties with landowners unwilling to grant rights-of-way, political wrangling, and funds lost is bureaucratic shuffling. In spite of this, however, much of the route was cleared and blazed, and signs and parking areas were developed. Gaps in the route continue to be used on an informal basis, as has been the case for generations.

Plans to build the trail on the Virginia side continue to be resurrected

Atop Clinch Mountain the Trail of the Lonesome Pine passes under rocky shelves.

periodically, and there are completed sections in the Jefferson National Forest.

The link given here runs along the western edge of Hawkins County, Tennessee. Other sections in Hancock and Grainger Counties are also open.

How to Get There

The northern end of this segment is reached from Weber City, Virginia. Turn from US-23 southwest onto VA-614; follow Poor Valley through Yuma and Kermit communities; cross the state line and turn right at 16.2 miles from Weber City. There are signs for the trail and a small parking area on this country lane.

To reach the segment from its southern end, take Highway 70 from Rogersville, Tennessee, toward Sneedville. At the crest of Clinch Mountain, 9.7 miles from the US-11-W/70 junction, paths lead to the summit and to the old fire tower on this knob. The path along the crest is still passable, but is difficult. In summer snakes abound. Yellow painted blazes mark the way northeastward along the crest, and there is a usable shelter near the fire tower.

The Trail

From the northern end, white blazes for the footpath lead over a fence stile to begin a diagonal ascent of Clinch Mountain. The crest is reached after about 1 mile of steady climbing.

At the top, the marked path leads southwesterly along the sharp spine of the summit. Detours are occasionally required for fallen trees, but otherwise the first few miles are in the moderate range of difficulty. There are pastoral views of quiet valleys and small farms. The crest, thrust upward eons ago, has unusual geological formations. One side of the mountain is sandstone and the other is limestone. Along the summit, rock strata from the eastern side has ridden upward, creating numerous ledges that overhang the path and form natural shelters.

Hunting and game paths have followed the summit of Clinch Mountain for centuries, and it can still be followed with or without blazes. This route has not been heavily used in recent years, however, and the degree of difficulty increases roughly in proportion to the distance from the nearest road.

There is no water on the trail. Camping is limited to designated sites, or permission of land owners.

Most of the walking is in the moderate range, but due to detours and primitive nature of much of the route, it should be rated difficult. The trail can be followed for several miles, generally for as far as the hiker's time and interest allow.

More Virginia Trails

Little Stoney Creek Trail
Length: 2-3 miles, one way—Easy.

The Little Stoney Creek Trail is located in the Jefferson National Forest near Dungannon, Virginia. Beginning at the Hanging Rock Recreation Area, it follows an old railroad bed along Little Stoney Creek to two separate waterfalls. The route is an easy creek side stroll of 2-3 miles, and offers beautiful scenery.

How to Get There

Located in northeastern Scott County, Virginia, the Hanging Rock Recreation area is on VA-72, 2.6 miles north of Dungannon. Dungannon can be approached via VA-65 (where VA-72 intersects) from US-23, or from Coeburn on US-58 Alternate.

Several secondary routes are also possible, and one particularly scenic route takes VA-71 north from Gate City. It turns left onto VA-680 just before entering Nickelsville, and winds through the countryside to the Clinch River and Dungannon. This route passes small mountain farms, the Twin Springs High School, and Bush's Mill.

The trail and falls can also be approached from their upper end by graveled country lanes. Roughly midway between the Hanging Rock Recreation Area entrance and Coeburn, Route 664 turns west from VA-72. Turn left onto Route 700 in about one mile; then turn left again onto Route 701, in slightly over a mile. The upper trail access to the waterfalls is near the creek crossing, on the left; and it is reached in less than ½ mile.

The Trail

The trail head at Hanging Rock Recreation Area is at the end of the gravel lane from VA-72. (In winter when the gate is closed, it is 0.4 mile from the pavement.) Yellow painted blazes and a gate mark the beginning of the hiker path, which is to the right of the picnic tables. The trail follows an

A fisherman wets a line below the upper falls on the Little Stoney Creek Trail.

old narrow gauge railroad bed near the shallow stream on the lower part of the route. It is clear, well maintained and fairly easy strolling most of the way.

Coal mines once operated in the lower part of the gorge, and their portals may be spotted on the ridge sides. There are steep walls along the gorge, along with mixed hardwoods, and numerous varieties of ferns and wildflowers. The stream has many small cascades and pools where native Brook Trout can be seen.

There are footbridges, concrete stepping stones and set stone steps at the creek crossings and steeper sections.

The first falls can be reached in less than an hour by walking at a steady, comfortable pace. The estimated distance is 2 miles. The lower falls are in the 50 foot range, and another ½ mile upstream the second falls are reached. There is a large pool beneath them, which is popular as a swimming hole on summer weekends.

Above the falls the footpath continues over footbridges to the upper parking lot. From this point it is possible to follow a combination of gravel lanes and marked hiker trails all the way to the observation tower atop High Knob, a hike in the 17 mile range.

Devil's Fork Trail
3 miles one way estimate—Moderate difficulty.

The Devil's Fork Trail is a primitive, unmarked path up Devil's Fork Creek to small waterfalls and the Devil's Bathtub. The creek has native Brook Trout. It would be easy walking except for the numerous stream fords. Height of the water determines how difficult the trail is. The walk is not recommended during rainy periods.

Road approach to trail: Turn north onto the paved road, following Stoney Creek upstream, from Fort Blackmore, Virginia. After several miles, the road enters the Jefferson National Forest and turns to gravel just beyond a good bridge across the main Stoney Creek. (The rough road climbs the mountain to near High Knob). A short distance on the left a Forest Service right-of-way turns beside an old barn, goes through an old field, and reaches the Devil's Fork branch of the stream in less than ¼ mile. From there, rough fishing paths continue upstream. This is the trail: just follow the stream.

During hard times many years ago, a family is supposed to have lived under the overhanging rock ledges of the gorge. Old coal mining equipment and slope mine portals line the lower part of the gorge. The walk is dark and moist, since the route goes through dense hardwood forest and laurel thickets. At about 3 miles (estimated), unusual hollowed-out boulders, worn away by years of rushing water and resembling an old fashioned bath tub are reached. This is the "Devil's Bathtub." A small waterfall is just ahead, and the path becomes impassable above this point.

Roaring Branch Trail
12 miles, one way estimate—Moderate.

The Roaring Branch Trail is a woodland walk along the spine of Stone Mountain. Beginning near the confluence of Roaring Branch and Powell River, between Appalachia and Big Stone Gap, it leads southwest to the Cave Springs Recreation Area in Lee County. In addition to regrowth native hardwoods, there is a stand of virgin hemlocks along the walk, according to the U.S. Forest Service.

How to Get There

Road access points are from either side of Stone Mountain. The four main ones are:

1. **US-23 Business**: The trail turns west from Business 23 beside Roaring Branch, between railroad underpasses, about midway between Appalachia and Big Stone Gap.

2. **Cave Springs Recreation Area**: Approximately 12 miles west of Big Stone Gap on US-58 Alternate, VA-621/622 turns right, and a sign points to the recreation area. The trail heads northeast from the parking area.

3. **Olinger Gap**: To meet the trail at about its midpoint, turn from Alternate US-58 onto VA-622 at approximately 6 miles from Big Stone Gap. VA-621 is intersected in just over 1 mile. Follow 621 for about ½ mile west, to the Olinger Community; turn right, returning to VA-622; cross the railroad tracks and start up mountain. From the last junction, drive 2.2 miles and park at the turnaround, just past an old barn. The trail is on the Stone Mountain crest, about ¾ mile along an old road.

4. **Keokee Lake Recreation Area**: The opposite side of Olinger Gap can be reached by a more difficult route. From US-23 Business, just south of Appalachia, turn onto VA-68 toward Keokee and Exeter; turn onto VA-623 to the lake. A rough path from the parking area leads around the western side of the lake and up the mountain to the Roaring Branch Trail near Olinger Gap.

The Trail

The Roaring Branch Trail, beginning from Powell River beside US-23 Business, ascends Stone Mountain in a southwesterly direction along the left bank of the small stream. There are cascades from the stony slopes. The brook may roar during flooding, but normally it only whispers enough to soften the sounds of traffic on the road below.

The cool, verdant area at the bottom of the hill attracts picnickers with low aesthetic values. They leave a sorry mess of Budweiser and Mountain Dew cans and Twinky and Big Mac wrappers.

Great effort was expended in developing this trail. There are rock steps up the steep face for several hundred yards. Fortunately, those too lazy to clean up after themselves are apparently too lazy to climb the hill as well, so their trash concentrates near the road.

The trail doesn't have painted blazes along the route, but instead uses them at points where the path makes sharp turns or the route isn't obvious (such as junctions with secondary trails). These yellow markings appear as a single patch to alert the walker, then as a double blaze at the turn or hazard.

The branch is reduced to a trickle in about 1 mile, and the path turns higher along the ridges. Returning to the stream a short distance later, the flow is reduced to a marsh with seeps and wet weather springs. From the boggy area, the trail ascends gradually along a high plateau for a mile or so, past a grove of great old hemlocks.

Trail conditions along the walk vary from a single file, primitive footpath to wide avenues that were once roads. At about 3.5-4 miles from the highway, the High Butte area is reached where side trails lead out to rocky cliffs overlooking the Powell River Valley. Care should be taken when exploring these spurs and game trails, since there are sheer dropoffs near the summit.

Olinger Gap is roughly the mid-point and can be distinguished by a wide vehicle track heading diagonally down the southern slope. There is also a large metal U.S. Forest Service stake set amid trees with red painted bands around them. The road down the south slope from here is clear and easy to follow. The access trail to the Keokee side is a bit more iffy, especially during weed season.

This area has been designated as a Special Management Area by the U.S. Forest Service. Perhaps this will result in additional emphasis on recreational trails in the vicinity.

According to area oldtimers, the trail along the Stone Mountain summit was once used heavily and could be walked all the way from Big Stone Gap to the Cumberland Gap. Now the developed trail extends for about 12 miles along a strip of Jefferson National Forest and ends at Cave Springs. The path can be picked up again near Ewing, Virginia, as a horse trail traveling for several miles along the Virginia/Kentucky lines in the Cumberland Gap National Park area.

Smaller cascades, between two larger waterfalls on Little Stoney Creek, provide relief from summer heat.

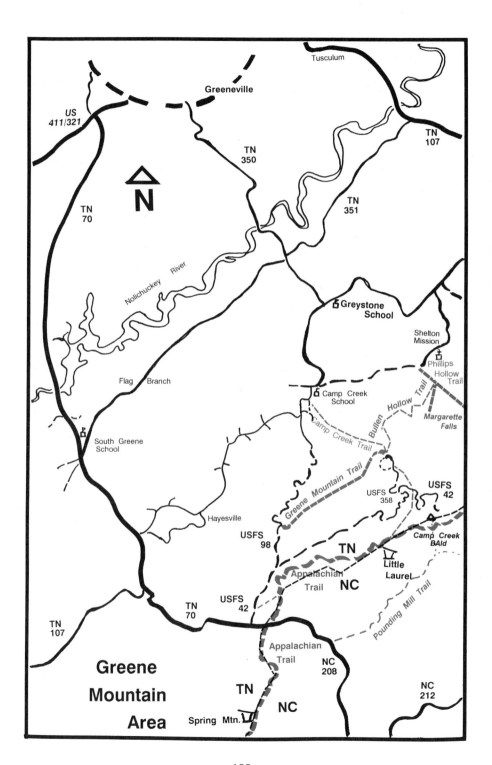

Tusculum

Greeneville

US
411/321

TN
350

TN
70

TN
107

TN
351

$\hat{N}$
N

Nolichuckey River

Greystone
School

Shelton
Mission

Phillips
Hollow
Trail

Flag   Branch

Camp Creek
School

Camp Creek Trail

Bullen Hollow Trail

Margarette
Falls

South Greene
School

Greene Mountain Trail

USFS
358

USFS
42

Hayesville

USFS
98

TN

Camp Creek
BAld

Appalachian
Trail

Little
Laurel

NC

TN
70

USFS
42

Pounding Mill Trail

TN
107

Appalachian
Trail

NC
208

NC
212

Greene
Mountain
Area

TN

NC

Spring Mtn.

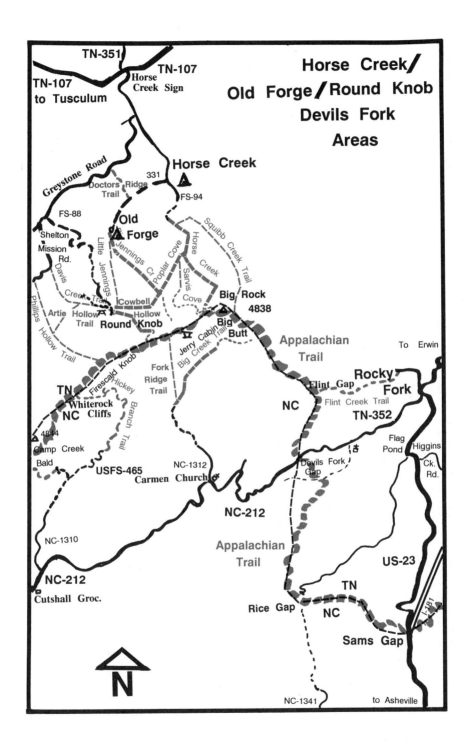

Horse Creek/
Old Forge/Round Knob
Devils Fork
Areas

TN-351

TN-107

TN-107
to Tusculum

Horse
Creek Sign

Greystone Road

Horse Creek

331

Doctors Ridge
Trail

FS-94

FS-88

Old
Forge

Shelton
Mission
Rd.

Squibb Creek Trail

Little Jennings

Jennings Cr

Poplar Cove

Horse Creek

Davis Creek Trail

Cowbell
Hollow

Sarvis
Cove

Big Rock
4838

Phillips Hollow Trail

Artie Hollow
Trail

Round Knob

Jerry Cabin

Big
Butt

Appalachian
Trail

To Erwin

Firescald Knob

Hickey Branch Trail

Fork
Ridge
Trail

Big Creek Trail

Flint Gap

Flint Creek Trail

Rocky
Fork

TN

Whiterock
NC   Cliffs

NC

TN-352

4844

Camp Creek
Bald

USFS-465

NC-1312

Carmen Church

Devils Fork
Gap

Flag
Pond

Higgins

Ck.
Rd.

NC-1310

NC-212

Appalachian
Trail

US-23

NC-212

Cutshall Groc.

Rice Gap

TN

NC

Sams Gap

I-181

NC-1341

to Asheville

N

—189—

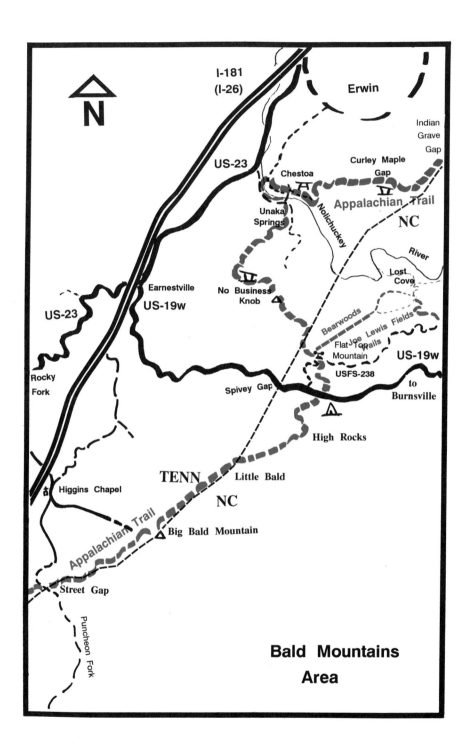

Bald Mountains
Area

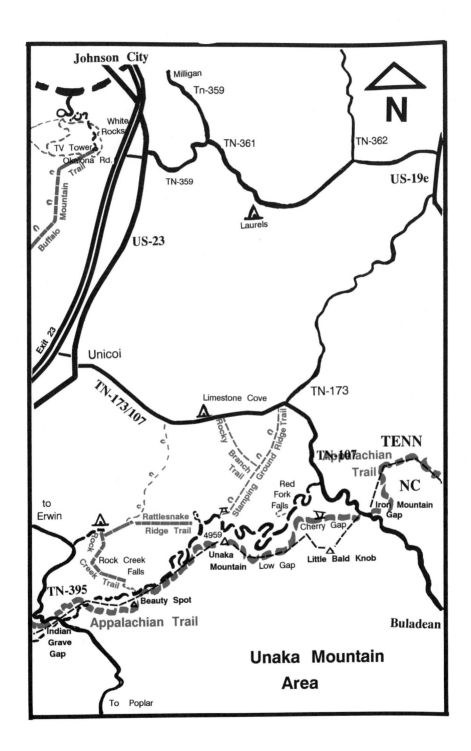

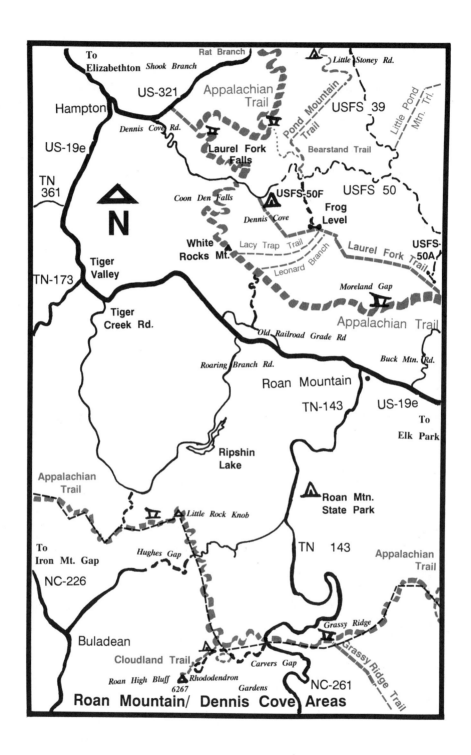

Roan Mountain/ Dennis Cove Areas

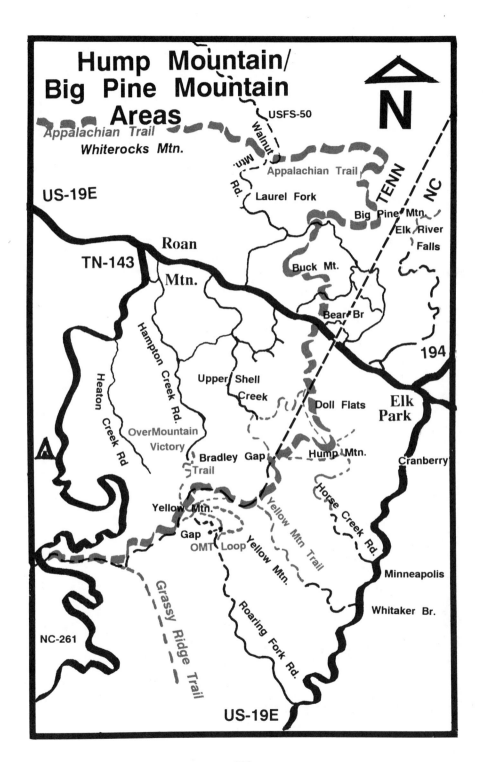

Hump Mountain/ Big Pine Mountain Areas

Appalachian Trail

Whiterocks Mtn.

USFS-50

Walnut Mtn. Rd.

Appalachian Trail

Laurel Fork

TENN

NC

US-19E

Big Pine Mtn.

Elk River Falls

Roan

TN-143

Mtn.

Buck Mt.

Bear Br

194

Hampton Creek Rd.

Upper Shell Creek

Doll Flats

Elk Park

Heaton Creek Rd

OverMountain Victory

Bradley Gap Trail

Hump Mtn.

Cranberry

Yellow Mtn.

Gap

OMT Loop

Yellow Mtn.

Yellow Mtn Trail

Horse Creek Rd.

Minneapolis

Whitaker Br.

NC-261

Grassy Ridge Trail

Roaring Fork Rd.

US-19E

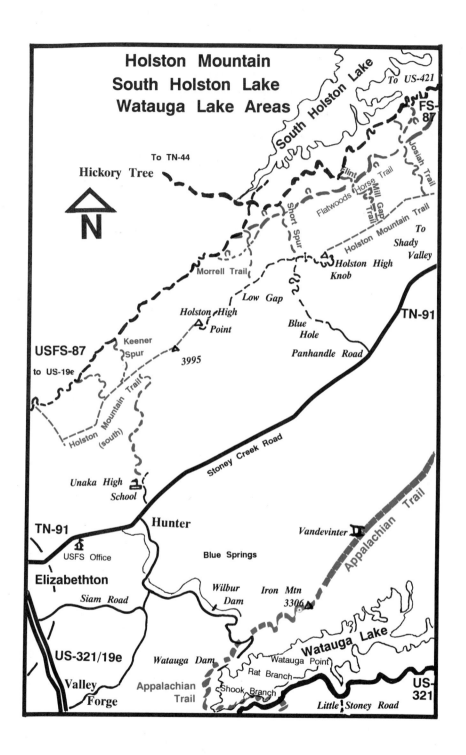

Holston Mountain
South Holston Lake
Watauga Lake Areas

South Holston Lake

To US-421

FS-87

Flint

Mill Gap Trail

Josiah Trail

To TN-44

Flatwoods Horse Trail

Hickory Tree

N

Short Spur

Holston Mountain Trail

To
Shady
Valley

Holston High
Knob

Morrell Trail

Low Gap

Blue
Hole

TN-91

Holston High
Point

Keener
Spur

3995

Panhandle Road

USFS-87

to US-19e

Holston Mountain Trail
(south)

Stoney Creek Road

Unaka High
School

Hunter

Vandevinter

Appalachian Trail

TN-91

Blue Springs

USFS Office

Elizabethton

Wilbur
Dam

Iron Mtn
3306

Siam Road

Watauga Lake

US-321/19e

Watauga Dam

Watauga Point

Rat Branch

US-321

Valley
Forge

Appalachian
Trail

Shook Branch

Little Stoney Road

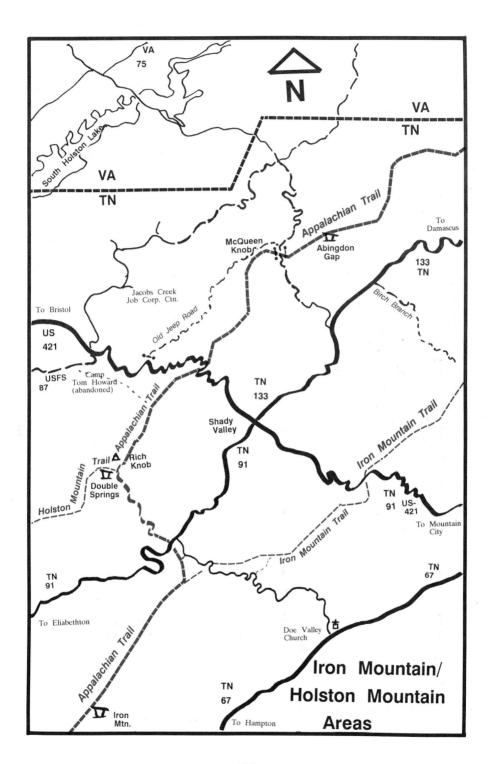

Iron Mountain/
Holston Mountain
Areas

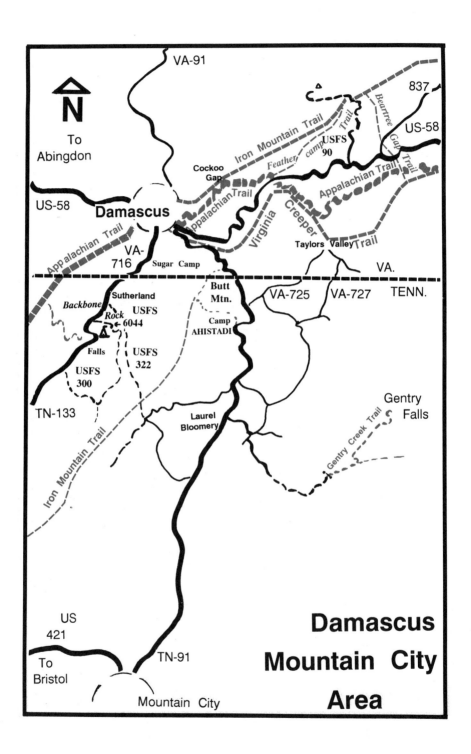

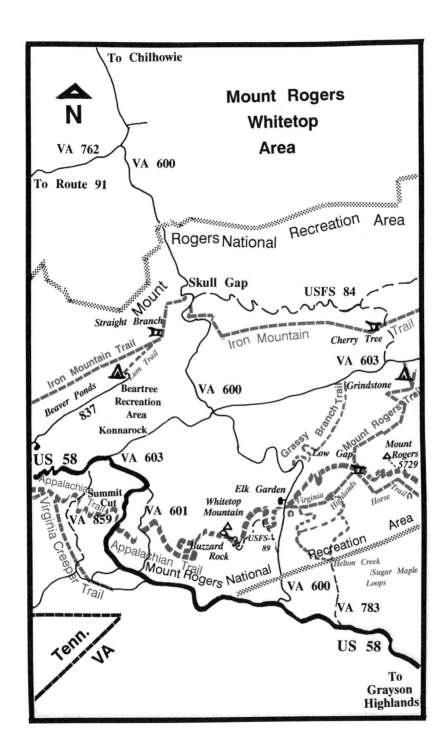

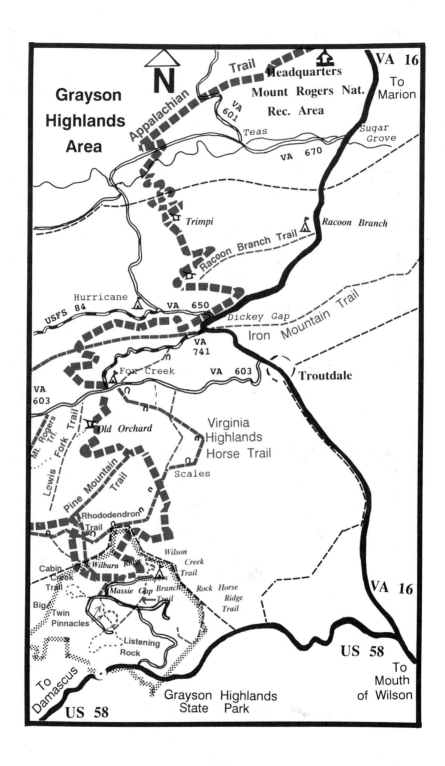